BOLIVIA

POLITICS IN LATIN AMERICA
A HOOVER INSTITUTION SERIES

General Editor, **Robert Wesson**

Copublished with Hoover Institution Press,
Stanford University, Stanford, California

BOLIVIA

Past, Present, and Future of Its Politics

Robert J. Alexander

PRAEGER SPECIAL STUDIES • PRAEGER SCIENTIFIC

Library of Congress Cataloging in Publication Data

Alexander, Robert Jackson, 1918–
    Bolivia: past, present, and future of its politics.

    (Politics in Latin America)
    Bibliography: p.
    Includes index.
    1. Bolivia–Politics and government.   2. Bolivia–
History.   I. Title.   II. Series.
F3321.A43   984   81–22661
ISBN 0–03–061762–6   AACR2

984
A377

*The Hoover Institution on War, Revolution and Peace,
founded at Stanford University in 1919 by the late President
Herbert Hoover is an interdisciplinary research center for
advanced study on domestic and international affairs in the
twentieth century. The views expressed in its publications
are entirely those of the authors and do not necessarily
reflect the views of the staff, officers, or Board of Overseers
of the Hoover Institution.*

Published in 1982 by Praeger Publishers
CBS Educational and Professional Publishing
a Division of CBS, Inc.
521 Fifth Avenue, New York, New York 10175 U.S.A.

23456789   145   987654321

Printed in the United States of America

To
James and Mabel Street

FOREWORD by Robert Wesson

This volume is part of the Hoover Institution-Praeger Politics in Latin America series. These studies are planned to provide a factual background on the politics and problems of all the republics to the south, a set of nation monographs supplemented by studies of international and regional problems.

After the volumes on Central America by Thomas Anderson, Panama by Steve Ropp, and Paraguay by Paul Lewis, it is appropriate to have a study of the most agitated and perhaps most picturesque country of Latin America. Bolivia is known for bleak scenery, stolid Indians, production of tin and cocaine, and coups, about 200 at the latest count. Its politics are inscrutable, but there may be no one who understands them better than Robert J. Alexander.

PREFACE

About a quarter of a century ago I had published one of the first books about the Bolivian National Revolution. In the intervening years I have maintained my interest in and concern with Bolivian events through visits to the country, the unique opportunities presented by an exchange program which Rutgers University had for many years with two Bolivian universities, and in other ways. Therefore, when Robert Wesson of the Hoover Institution asked if I would be willing to write the volume on Bolivia for a series that the institution was preparing on various Latin American countries, I was most happy to do so.

The current volume is broader in scope, although perhaps smaller in volume, than my earlier work. Although perforce this book deals at some length with the Bolivian National Revolution, the most important event in Bolivia's twentieth-century history, it goes considerably beyond that subject. It seeks to give the reader an overall view and, hopefully, an understanding of Bolivia. It also attempts to recount how the country got to where it is today.

I am indebted to the people who have helped this book become a reality. I owe much to the people, Bolivians and others, who over many years have submitted to my persistent questioning about their country and events transpiring in it. They would be too numerous to name here. Naturally, they bear no responsibility for what appears herein, such responsibility being wholly mine.

Thanks are extended to Robert Wesson for the invitation to write this volume, giving me the opportunity to review my own information, thoughts, and feelings about Bolivia.

Finally, as is always the case, I owe a debt to my wife for preparing the index and, as always, for her patience with my preoccupation with Bolivia when she may well have thought that I'd be better occupied doing something else.

Rutgers University
New Brunswick, New Jersey
December 1981

CONTENTS

LIST OF ACRONYMS

AID   Agency for International Development

ADN   Accion Democratica Nacionalista
             (Nationalist Democratic Action)

COB   Central Obrera Boliviana
             (Bolivian Labor Confederation)

COMIBOL   Corporacion Minera de Bolivia
             (Bolivian Mining Corporation)

ECLA   Economic Commission for Latin America

FPN   Frente Popular Nacionalista
             (Nationalist Popular Front)

FSTM   Federación Sindical de Trabajadores Mineros
             (Mine Workers Federation)

FUB   Federación Universitaria Boliviana
             (Bolivian University Students Federation)

MIR   Movimiento de Izquierda Revolucionaria
             (Movement of the Revolutionary Left)

MNR   Movimiento Nacionalista Revolucionario
             (Nationalist Revolutionary Movement)

MNRH   Movimiento Nacionalista Revolucionario-Historico
             (Historic Nationalist Revolutionary Movement)

MNRI   Movimiento Nacionalista Revolucionario de Izquierda
             (Nationalist Revolutionary Movement of the Left)

OPEC	Organization of Petroleum Exporting Countries
PCB	Partido Comunista de Bolivia (Communist Party of Bolivia)
PIR	Partido de Izquierda Revolucionaria (Party of the Revolutionary Left)
POR	Partido Obrero Revolucionario (Revolutionary Labor Party)
PRA	Partido Revolucionario Autentico (Authentic Revolutionary Party)
PRIN	Partido Revolucionario de la Izquierda Nacionalista (Revolutionary Party of the Nationalist Left)
PSOB	Partido Socialista Obrero Boliviana (Bolivian Socialist Labor Party)
PURS	Partido de Unificacion Republicana Socialista (Party of Republican Socialist Unification)
YPFB	Yacimientos Petroleos Fiscales Bolivianos (Bolivian Government Petroleum Reserves)

INTRODUCTION

The average street dealer in cocaine in any U.S. city may know more about Bolivia than do the great majority of his compatriots. He may be aware of the fact that what he is selling probably originated there, and will have some judgment as to the quality of the Bolivian product. A somewhat more sophisticated North American may know that Bolivia has long been closely associated with tin. A history buff may possibly be aware of the fabulous mountain of silver at Potosí that poured riches into the coffers of the Spanish king for more than two centuries.

In a word, the average U.S. citizen is very ignorant of Bolivia. One might say that there is no special reason why the average person should be particularly knowledgable about that country. Bolivia is not a particularly powerful nation, economically, diplomatically, militarily, or in any other way. The fate of the United States has not depended on what happens or does not happen there. Nor has Bolivia (strangely enough) ever caught on among Americans as a tourist attraction.

However, this ignorance is a great shame. There are many attributes of Bolivia that should be of interest to the average North American. Bolivia is a country possessing some of the most striking and awe-inspiring scenery anywhere on earth. It has one of the most "different" populations to be found anywhere in the Americas. The Indian population of the republic (which includes more than half of the Bolivians) still lives to a considerable degree in the way they have for innumerable centuries and the Indian women still wear clothing unlike that found anywhere else in the world.

Bolivia is of significance to the United States far beyond being a center of potential tourism. It contains within its frontiers very large mineral and agricultural resources that have only begun to be explored and exploited, and are of great importance to the United States, including such commodities as tin and scarcer minerals like antimony, bismuth, and tungsten as well as petroleum.

The significance of Bolivia is considerable because of its strategic geographical location. It is almost in the center of South America and borders on five other nations: Chile, Peru, Brazil, Paraguay, and Argentina. Although not itself a powerful country, it is one that its neighbors would not care to see in the hands of any other powerful country. Nor would the United States like to have Bolivia in the hands of a hostile power. Once in recent years the possible political and military significance of Bolivia was underscored when in 1967 Ernesto (Ché) Guevara sought to establish a guerrilla base in the eastern part of

Bolivia from which to maintain a center of operations to function not only in that republic but in all of the neighboring ones as well.

However, for those who believe in political democracy and social justice, Bolivia has further significance. Although it has had little real experience with a democratic political system, Bolivia has for long had valiant and persistent political leaders who have fought for the establishment of democracy. Furthermore, Bolivia has undergone one of the most fundamental revolutionary experiences of any of the countries of the Western Hemisphere. Occurring between 1952 and 1964, the revolution had as one of its principal objectives to right the wrongs done to the Indian inhabitants of the republic for the more than four centuries since the arrival of the Spanish conquerors.

Unfortunately, although the Bolivian National Revolution at first seemed to give promise of establishing a political system in which the presidency would be transferred from one incumbent to the other by more or less democratic elections, this did not in fact come to pass. Rather, the 12-year period of revolutionary government presided over by the Movimiento Nacionalista Revolucionario has been succeeded by a series of presidents from the armed forces, which has precedents in terms of Bolivian militarism only in the first half of the nineteenth century.

The chapters that follow present both the background and the current state of Bolivian government and politics. Chapter 1 discusses the geographical ambience of Bolivia and the nature of the country's population. These two factors are of particular significance in determining the nature of Bolivian politics both in the past and at the present time. This discussion is followed by a survey in Chapter 2 of the country's economy, which also is an essential factor in explaining the nature of the nation's political system and how it functions.

However, to a considerable degree, the approach will be a historical one since it is impossible really to understand the current state of affairs without a comprehension of the historical background. This is even truer of Bolivia than it may be of some other countries.

So, the five chapters following deal with the historical development of Bolivia. Chapter 3 treats first the Indian civilization that existed before the arrival of the Spanish conquistadores and then the period during which Bolivia was a Spanish colony. The first century of the nation's independence is studied in Chapter 4. This discussion is followed by a survey in Chapter 5 of the country's greatest single catastrophe, the Chaco War, and its impact on the country's society and polity. Chapter 6 outlines the nature, accomplishments, and shortcomings of the Bolivian National Revolution, generally conceded to be one of the three most fundamentally revolutionary developments in Latin America in the twentieth century, and Chapter 7 deals with what has happened since the end of the revolutionary regime in 1964.

Chapter 8 analyzes the contemporary relevance of what has gone before, presenting the major factors that have determined the government and politics of the country in the early 1980s, and Chapter 9 discusses the impact of foreign relations. In conclusion Chapter 10 speculates—hesitantly—on the future perspective of Bolivia's political system. The Bibliographical Note that follows contains full bibliographic information for the references quoted in the text.

BOLIVIA

1

THE LAND AND THE PEOPLE

Bolivia is a land of great contrasts and many unknowns. It is a "Spanish-speaking" country in which for the majority of the people Spanish is not their native language. Although a tropical nation, the majority of the people live in a temperate, if not frigid, climate. It is a country with some of the highest mountains in the world and major rivers that drop in altitude so slowly that their waters move with great sluggishness. In this nation of vast natural resources, the great mass of the people are abysmally poor.

There is no agreement even among experts concerning some of the most fundamental facts about the country. There is no consensus even on its total area. The size of the Bolivian population is at best an educated guess. Many if not most of the natural resources of the country remain to be discovered. Bolivia's long frontiers and the impossibility of policing them adequately result in only a guess at the country's exports and imports—statistics about which most Latin American governments are quite well informed because of the importance of taxes on them to state revenues.

BOLIVIA'S TERRITORY

Some of the facts about Bolivia and its history are clear. It is certain that the country in the last part of the twentieth century covers less than half of the territory it claimed upon independence in 1825. Even so, Bolivia remains a nation equal in size to France and Spain combined, and is the sixth largest national territory in Latin America, surpassed only by Brazil, Argentina, Mexico, Peru, and Colombia.

During the first century and a half of its existence as a sovereign state, Bolivia lost territory to all of its neighbors. To the west, Chile in the 1879–83 War of the Pacific seized 46,233 square miles, including all Bolivian territory on the Pacific Ocean. In the northeast at the turn of the twentieth century, Brazil, in an operation resembling the seizure of Texas by migrants from the United States about half a century earlier, took over 189,353 square miles in the Acre region. In addition, Argentina acquired 65,924 square miles of what had been southern Bolivia, and Peru obtained 96,527 square miles in the northeastern part of the country. Finally, in the Chaco War of the 1930s Bolivia lost an estimated 94,018 square miles of its southeastern territory to its fifth neighbor, Paraguay.

Thus, it is estimated that when it emerged to independence Bolivia claimed a territory of some 904,052 square miles, and although there is no firm agreement to this day concerning just how much it was left with, it is clear that Bolivia constitutes less than half of what it began with. The total area of Bolivia in the last part of the twentieth century is somewhere in the vicinity of 420,000 square miles. North to south, Bolivian territory extends at its greatest length to about 950 miles, while from east to west it is about 900 miles across at its widest point.

THE ALTIPLANO

Geographically Bolivia divides into three clearly distinct regions. The Andean area, with its two ranges of mountains and the great plateau in between, covers about one-fourth of the national territory but has over one-half of the population. The largest area is the Oriente, which is only a few hundred feet above sea level and covers nearly three-fourths of the country's area. Between the Andes and the Oriente lie the Yungas, the valleys that lead from the one to the other.

The Great Plateau of Bolivia, or the Altiplano as it is known, is created by two high ranges of the Andes. To the west is the Cordillera Occidental, which constitutes the present border with Chile. To the east is the Cordillera Real. Each of these mountain ranges is broken into sectors or segments, three in the western chain and five in the Cordillera Real.

The mountains in the Bolivian part of the Andes include many of the world's highest peaks. The Cordillera Occidental is said to average 16,500 feet in altitude, and for a hundred miles the Cordillera Real has an average height of 18,000 feet. There are very high mountains particularly in the Cordillera Real, including Chachacomani at 20,528 feet, Huayna Potosí at 20,407 feet, and Illimani at 21,325 feet, which looms majestically and breathtakingly over La Paz.

Between these two ranges, which begin at the "knot" at Apolobamba in southern Peru and extend beyond the southern border of Bolivia, is the Altiplano. It is about 520 miles long and between 80 and 100 miles wide. About

38,000 square miles out of a total of 50,000 square miles of the Altiplano are located within the Bolivian frontiers.

Some geologists have speculated that the Altiplano was once a great inland sea which spilled out to the East through the present Cochabamba Valley. However, that theory is not as popular today. In any case, the Altiplano consists largely of sedimentary rocks washed down in the far distant past by rivers from the high mountains, and continuing to be deposited by the strong and sometimes violent winds that sweep up and down the Altiplano today. This layer of sedimentary rock may be as much as 3,000 feet thick. These deposits are very fragile in nature, and the visitor may upon first acquaintance be startled to pick up what appears to be a rock and find that it will crumble into sandy earth.

At the north end of the Altiplano lies Lake Titicaca, which at 12,500 feet above sea level is one of the highest bodies of navigable water to be found anywhere on earth. Sovereignty over the lake is shared by Bolivia and Peru, and it forms part of the boundary between the two countries. It is about 138 miles long and 70 miles wide at its broadest point, covering (together with the 36 islands within it) some 3,500 square miles. Fabulous stories have been told about the lake being bottomless in some areas, and the Indians were said to believe that its waters found their way underground to the Pacific Ocean. In fact, however, the depth of the lake tends to be between 900 and 1,500 feet deep.

Lake Titicaca has a special place in the lore of both the Aymara and the Quechua Indians. It is said that the Incas originally came from there. And belief has it that the sun was born in the lake, and there decided to create the human race and its various subdivisions. Tradition also has it that the Incas, in a desperate effort to save some of their fabulous gold and silver treasures from the avaricious Spanish conquerors, dumped a large quantity of them in the lake at some point. Various attempts to search for this treasure have been in vain.

Lake Titicaca's water goes into the Desaguadero River, which flows for 200 miles to the south into the second largest lake of the Altiplano, Lake Poopo, which is about 20 miles wide and 56 miles long. It is a kind of Andean Dead Sea, having only a small outlet, the Lakahuira River, which goes underground not far from the lake, leaving the lake itself intensely salty. This salt has contaminated the land around and apparently accounts for the 3,220 square mile Uyuni salt deposits known as the Salares.

One traveling across the Altiplano cannot help but be awed by the beauty, the power, and sometimes the cruelty of nature. The high altitude and the relative scarcity of oxygen result in a startling clarity of vision in the high plateau. The startling grandeur of the great mountains, the higher ones snow-capped the year round, seems very close, no matter how far away one actually is. There is little in the Altiplano, except the mountains on its borders, to obstruct one's vision, while above the sky has a blueness that is not often seen in lower climes. Clouds are rare, except wisps that cling to some of the mountain tops.

The Altiplano itself is a very bare, brownish gray as far as one can see.

There are almost no trees in the great plateau, and in the southern part particularly, there are few other forms of plant life. Cultivation of the land occasionally provides a spot of color, but such breaks in the landscape are rare. Only around the edge of Lake Titicaca are there substantial areas where man has to some degree modified the visual pattern of nature.

The Altiplano is relatively arid and in some of the southern part is desert. Even where that is not the case, there is virtually no rain in the winter months of April to October, and relatively modest amounts fitfully in the other months. When it does rain, the porousness of the soil soon absorbs the dampness. Farming is understandably difficult.

The climate of the Altiplano is rigorous. Although during the day the direct rays of the sun provide warmth, and may impose a tan if not a sunburn upon the unwary, the Altiplano is almost unbearably cold at night, even in the "summertime." The cold winds that blow almost constantly assure this.

The high altitude and scarcity of oxygen in the Altiplano can afflict the visitor with *siroche* or altitude sickness. Most people who arrive freshly on the Altiplano will find that after three or four days at most they will be able to get along quite well in spite of the decrease in oxygen. Even so, it is wise to avoid strenuous exercise. Some doctors advise that it is not wise for lowlanders who are afflicted with heart trouble to go to the Altiplano.

One theory has it that siroche is caused not so much by the height or oxygen scarcity of the Altiplano as by the abruptness of most travelers' transfer from lower areas to the high plateau. One way to avoid siroche, therefore, is to come up to the highlands via the railroad, either from Arica, which takes 24 hours to reach La Paz, or from Antofagasta, which takes a day and a half to two days. The natives of the Altiplano, both Indian and mestizo, have largely adapted physically to the conditions of altitude and shortage of oxygen. The chest cavity and lungs of the average highland Bolivian are substantially larger than those of natives of a lower altitude.

LA PAZ

The capital, and by far the largest city in Bolivia, La Paz is located in a crevice of the Altiplano at the head of a decline that leads first to the Yungas and ultimately to the eastern lowlands. To a newcomer, it is startling to arrive at the ridge of the Altiplano and suddenly to see a thousand feet below a modestly large city spread out.

Until the early 1970s it took over an hour to get from the airport on the Altiplano to the center of La Paz, via a rather narrow road with infinite curves on its way down to the metropolis. Subsequently, however, a wide highway, with considerably less winding and twisting was constructed to cover most of the distance from the Altiplano to the capital city.

La Paz is a spectacular city. Its main street cuts directly through the center of the town, sloping more or less gently downward for a mile or two in the direction of the valley many miles below and then dropping much more steeply. Off in the distance—but seeming much closer—is the excruciatingly beautiful Mount Illimani. Snow covered and sometimes with wisps of cloud around its peak, the mountain seems to hover over the city. From up on the western side of the city crevice can also be seen the tips of other mountains. But one seems to see virtually all of Illimani, and it gives a special character to the Bolivian capital.

From each side of the main thoroughfare, streets rise precipitously up the sides of the crevice in which the city is located. For some blocks there are office buildings, and a little way up the eastern side of the crevice there is the Plaza Murillo, with the presidential palace, cathedral, and other public buildings. But beyond this area are the homes of the humbler citizens of the town. They may be of stone, adobe, or a combination. The "posher" residential area of the more well-to-do is located further down the hill, on the way to the Yungas. There, too, are the principal military installations.

THE ORIENTE

The Oriente or eastern part of Bolivia occupies about 70 percent of the territory of the republic. However, much of the region is virtually unoccupied. Only since the early 1950s have significant and consistent efforts been made to develop the area economically.

The Oriente, for practical purposes, divides into two segments. To the north, most of the territory of the departments of Pando and Beni is covered by tropical forests that in the early 1950s covered about half of the country's territory. To the south is a region of open woodland and savannas, particularly in the department of Santa Cruz, which has since the early 1950s been the area of most rapid economic diversification and development.

In the northern part of the Oriente the forest coverage is quite diverse. It includes a great variety of deciduous and evergreen hardwoods, but distance from potential markets and almost impossible impediments to travel have prevented the commercial exploitation of most of these. In the past, only rubber, quinine, and Brazil nuts have been harvested to any commercial extent.

Bolivia's most important rivers are in the Oriente. The northern part of the area, the Beni Plain, is drained principally by the Beni and Mamoré Rivers, which are part of the Amazon system. The major river of the central and southern sections of the Oriente is the Pilcomayo, which flows into the Rio de la Plata system in the southern part of the continent.

Although the eastern part of the country includes territory sloping down from 1,500 feet to 300 feet, in much of the territory the slope is exceedingly gentle. This, plus the very heavy rainfall during certain periods of the year, is the reason why the Beni, Orton, Mamoré, and Madre de Dios rivers and their tributaries are subject to frequent flooding. As a result of this, much of the area is totally inundated during half the year, and throughout the year the principal means of transport, aside from aviation, is by the rivers. Since the revolution in 1952 roads have penetrated the periphery of the area and air transport has been developed as a means of getting meat from there to the highland parts of the republic. The drier parts of the Beni are the most important cattle-producing area of Bolivia.

The departments of Santa Cruz and Chuquisaca in the southeast, where the forests are less dense and there is a large savannah region, lend themselves to tropical agriculture, which has expanded markedly during the last three decades. Santa Cruz is also the center of the country's oil industry. The two southern departments of the Oriente contain the small portion of the Gran Chaco, which was left to Bolivia after the Chaco War with Paraguay in the early 1930s. They also are the location of large iron deposits on the Bolivian side of the Paraguay River, near the Brazilian city of Corumbá, which have still not been exploited. Since the area has never been thoroughly explored and charted, it may well be that it contains other mineral resources.

The only two important urban centers in the Oriente are Trinidad in the northern part of the area and Santa Cruz in the south, the capital of the department of the same name. The development of Trinidad is hampered by the fact that the city is peculiarly subject to floods during the part of the year when the rivers of the Oriente are particularly high, and sometimes the larger part of the city is inundated. In contrast, Santa Cruz has since the 1950s become a boom town as a result of the economic development of its hinterland due to the opening of the Santa Cruz-Cochabamba highway a year after the beginning of the 1952 Bolivian National Revolution.

THE YUNGAS

The Aymara word *Yungas* is used in Bolivia for the valleys that lie between the Altiplano and the Oriente. The most important of these are those that lie below La Paz; the valley of Cochabamba, the Sucre region, and Tarija.

The Yungas contained about one-third of the population of Bolivia before the 1952 revolution. However, there has been substantial migration from the valleys to the Oriente as a result of the economic development programs of the revolutionary government and its successors, and as a result, the area probably contains a somewhat smaller proportion of the republic's total number of inhabitants at the present time.

The Yungas have generally a temperate or semitropical climate. Their altitude varies from 3,000 to 6,500 feet above sea level and the region is one of high humidity. Much of it is still covered with forest of great heterogeneity. Among the trees found there are mahogany and cedar as well as walnut, laurel, jacaranda, and the quina tree, from which quinine is made. Cocoa and coffee trees are cultivated there. There are also many kinds of shrubs and bushes, including sarsaparilla, maguey, and saffron as well as vilca, from which tannin can be extracted.

The Yungas are a region of very great fertility. Much of the food for the Altiplano urban areas is grown there, including a great variety of fruits, vegetables such as sweet potatoes, cucumbers, yucca, peanuts, and the pepper plant *aji*. The flowers that are sold in profusion in La Paz are grown there. The Yungas is also the center for the cultivation of coca, which has been grown by the Indians since pre-Columbian times and in recent years has achieved particular commercial importance.

Cochabamba, Sucre, and Tarija are the major urban centers of the area of the valleys. Cochabamba has a delightful Mediterranean-type climate and is the center of one of the nation's richest agricultural areas as well as one of the principal manufacturing centers. Since 1953 it has been the Western terminus of the Cochabamba-Santa Cruz Highway, which has given the city increased economic and political significance.

Sucre is the old colonial capital and still officially the capital of Bolivia, although the only branch of government there is the Supreme Court. It continues to have a certain colonial air about it.

Tarija is a city quite removed from the rest of the republic. It was not even a part of Bolivia when it achieved independence, being the only territory that the republic has gained (from Argentina) since its birth, in contrast to the losses in most other directions.

THE PEOPLE OF THE ALTIPLANO AND THE YUNGAS

Estimates concerning the total population of Bolivia vary considerably. However, a more or less reliable census in 1976 estimated the total to be 4,687,718, or approximately 4.85 people per square kilometer. The concentration of population varied from a high of 12.5 per square kilometer in the most thickly settled department, La Paz, to 0.55 per square kilometer in Pando, in the Oriente.

It has also been estimated that at least 53 percent of the total population of the country are still Indians. Since one's race tends to be determined in cultural terms rather than in those of ancestry, this would indicate that a majority of the country's inhabitants have Qurchua, Aymara, or some other Indian language as their native tongue and live according to Indian customs.

Certainly, the great majority of the people of the Altiplano and Yungas areas of Bolivia are Indians. The Altiplano was the first center of civilization in

South America, and the Indians are divided between the Aymara, who are generally thought to be the descendants of the founders of the first great civilization of the Andes, and the Quechua, at least some of whom are descended from colonists sent to the region during the centuries of domination of the Altiplano by the Incas. Quechua was the language of the Incas.

During the three centuries of the colonial era and the first century and a half of Bolivia's existence as an independent republic, the Indians fought to maintain control over at least a part of their land as well as to preserve their cultural identity—language, religion, and even dress.

The Indians found that the best way in which they could avoid, or at least mitigate, oppression at the hands of the whites and mestizos was to stay apart from them. Thus, many fled to the remoter parts of the Altiplano. The vast majority continued to speak their own languages and did not learn the Spanish of their rulers. Most stayed loyal to their pre-Columbian gods, although these were often hidden behind the guise of the Christian deity and the saints of the Roman Catholic Church.

The results of this centuries-long passive resistance—interspersed from time to time with violent uprisings—are evident today. The native language of a majority of the people of the Altiplano is still either Aymara or Quechua, and a substantial portion of the population still does not know how to converse in the official language of Bolivia, Spanish.

Most of the Indians of the Altiplano are peasants. Until 1952 the great majority were held in bondage to white or mestizo masters. Since the agrarian reform carried out by the Bolivian National Revolution they have been small landholders. This transformation has made the Indian peasant of the Altiplano very conservative. He continues to be averse to abandoning his ancient culture and is similarly reluctant to alter the way in which his ancestors for countless generations have cultivated the soil. Only very slowly has he adapted to changed circumstances to the degree of using some portions—larger or smaller, depending upon the community involved and the individual peasant—of his land for growing some crops for sale in the market while still cultivating most of it on a subsistence basis.

Since the revolution of the 1950s, the Indians have been a potent political force in Bolivia. During the period in which the Movimiento Nacionalista Revolucionario or Nationalist Revolutionary Movement (MNR) controlled the government (1952-64), the Indians were a major force defending the regime, but they have been a largely passive element in national politics since the overthrow of the MNR. They have been willing to support—or at least tolerate—any government that is willing to allow them continued ownership of their land. Ernesto (Che) Guevara learned this to his grief when he tried to enlist the peasants in a guerrilla campaign against the government of President René Barrientos in 1967.

Many Indians reside in the cities of the Altiplano. However, a substantial number have learned Spanish and tend to look upon themselves as *cholos*, rather than as pure Indians. A cholo is supposedly a mestizo, that is, a person with mixed Indian and European ancestry, although in the case of many of the urban cholos of Bolivia their ancestry is pure Indian and only their culture is an intermixture of the two strains.

The people of the Altiplano who are neither Indians nor cholos are officially "white." However, here again, culture and social position are more telling factors in determining one's ethnicity than actual blood strains. Miscegenation between the Spaniards and the Indians began with the first generation of conquistadores, most of whom never did bring their European spouses—if they had any—to the New World. Furthermore, although during the first two centuries of the colonial period there were substantial numbers of Spaniards resident in Bolivia—particularly in the silver mining city of Potosí—most had abandoned Upper Peru (the colonial name for Bolivia) before Simón Bolívar's armies brought about the country's separation from Spain in 1825. The people who remained as the Bolivian elite were the part-Spanish and part-Indian descendants of the conquistadores and other favored Spaniards who had received land grants from the crown or built up commercial enterprises in Upper Peru during the colonial period.

As a consequence, in late twentieth-century Bolivia, the majority of those classified as "whites" are in fact people of mixed ancestry. However, they are culturally an offshoot of European civilization. They speak and read the Spanish language, and follow customs in literature, art, music, and clothing that come from Europe or the United States.

The non-Indians of Bolivia, in spite of the pro-Indianism that has been the official ideology of all governments since 1952 (which, among other things, has made it impolite to use the word "Indian" instead of "peasants"), have a disdain, if not a contempt, for the Indian. Student rebels who frequently profess to speak on behalf of the indigenous people seldom if ever venture out into the countryside to establish real contacts with them. Even national political leaders who in fact have been responsible for giving the peasants most of the land of the Altiplano have found it difficult to realize that much more is needed before the Indians can be thoroughly integrated into the national life of Bolivia.

In addition to the traditional "whites" of mixed ancestry, there are relatively small numbers of people of more recent Old World origin who have settled in the Altiplano and the Yungas. Two important groups are of German origin, gentile and Jewish. A small number of German immigrants were attracted by the tin boom at the end of the last century and the beginning of this one to seek their fortunes in Bolivia. One president of the republic, Germán Busch, was the offspring of such a father. The Jewish immigrants, on the other hand, arrived for the most part in the 1930s, when that same President Germán Busch opened the country to Jewish refugees from Hitlerite persecution. Most of the Jewish immigrants came into the country ostensibly as "farmers," and in fact settled for the most part either in La Paz or Cochabamba. Corruption of appropriate Bolivian consular officials in Europe was often necessary to get one of the cherished visas. Busch's humanitarian gesture toward the Jews, most of them from Germany, was perhaps the best answer to those detractors of Busch who accused him of Fascist if not Nazi sympathies.

Some of the more recent immigrants from the Old World (who number at most a few tens of thousands) came from Asia, rather than Europe. As elsewhere in Latin America, a few Arabs made Bolivia their destination. They were mostly from the Palestine-Syria-Lebanon area. Most were businessmen, and were among the people who established a modern textile factory industry in the country. One Arab immigrant, Sr. Lechín, was the father of two sons, both named Juan, one of whom became leader of the Mine Workers Federation and vice-president of the republic, the other entered the armed forces and became the chief of general staff.

The people of the Yungas, like those of the Altiplano, are predominantly Indians who speak Quechua. They constitute between one-fourth and one-third of the total population of the country. Most are peasants and since the 1950s, small landowners.

The presence of so many Indians in the Yungas negates the old tale that the Altiplano Indian cannot adapt to life in the lower altitude regions. Even though the Altiplano Indians may have adapted physically to life in the rarified atmosphere of the High Plateau, they have found no difficulty in settling in the lower regions of the valleys. In recent decades, substantial numbers of people from the Yungas area have moved to still lower altitudes, becoming colonists in the newly opened regions of the Oriente.

The city of Cochabamba has a much more heterogeneous population than the rural sections of the valleys in Bolivia. There are Indians, but there are also cholos, "whites," and a leaven of recent European immigrants.

THE CHOLO MARKET WOMEN

Mention must be made of the cholo market women of La Paz and the other cities of the Altiplano and the Yungas. These redoubtable ladies conduct much of the country's retail trade, and are distinguished not only by their distinctive clothing but also by their political influence.

Although the market women of the principal cities are in their great majority undoubtedly of pure Indian ancestry from a biological point of view, they regard themselves, and are regarded by the rest of the community, as cholos. They are at least bilingual, speaking their own Indian language and Spanish.

These women are perhaps the most colorful members of the country's population. They wear many layers of skirts, each of a different color and so arranged that most of them can be seen, and a kind of shawl around their shoulders, in which they frequently secrete some of their possessions and sometimes carry their small offspring. Most distinctive of all is the headgear of the market women. It is of great variety, and to the *cognoscenti* indicates the part of the country from which they originate. These head adornments include brown derbies, high white-lacquered hats, headgear made to resemble the helmets worn by the conquistadores, and a variety of others. Perched atop the heads of their owners, the head adornments often set off fine gold or silver earrings, bracelets, and chains that are undoubtedly both of great value and a source of pride for the owners.

The market ladies have a reputation for sharp bargaining. Giving the impression that one of their sources of entertainment and interest is negotiation with prospective purchasers, they have developed to a fine art the process of appearing to be disdainful of the "paltry" sums offered by would-be buyers of their wares. However, they are not only able businesswomen, but are sometimes influential politicians. Their acquaintance with the general populace is wide, and they are strategically located to make known their discontent with policies and personalities of the regime currently in power. More than one government in recent decades has learned to its regret the danger of arousing the concerted opposition of the market women of La Paz.

THE PEOPLE OF THE ORIENTE

The population of the Eastern part of Bolivia is markedly different from that of the Altiplano and the Yungas. The proportion of whites and near-whites in the region has been markedly higher than in the other two sections of the country since the early colonial period. In addition, the Indian residents have until recent decades not been Aymara and Quechua speaking people like those in the Altiplano, but rather (in Santa Cruz and Chuquisaca) of the Guarani language, related to those who made up the indigenous population of Paraguay. In the northern departments of the Oriente, Pando, and Beni, many of the Indians were of Amazonian tribes that were still hunters and gatherers rather than settled agriculturalists.

Since the revolution of the 1950s, continuing efforts have been made by successive governments to settle people from the Altiplano and the Yungas in the Oriente, particularly in the southern part. Colonists from other parts of the country have been offered land of their own and have been given a modicum of help by the government to meet their needs until they could harvest their first crops.

These efforts have had considerable success. Hundreds of thousands of Indians have settled along the Cochabamba-Santa Cruz Highway and along other roads built out from it. Others have settled in the area centering on the city of

Santa Cruz. And some of the Indians who have moved into the Oriente in recent decades have come from Peru rather than from other parts of Bolivia. Thus the ethnic composition of the population of the Oriente has substantially altered during the last generation.

Among the colonists settled in the East have been several thousand people from Japan. Brought in during the 1950s, some came from the main islands of Japan, others from Okinawa, which was then still under U.S. control. As a result, at the time of their arrival, these immigrants were at first classified as Japanese and Okinawans, although with time, this distinction has receded in importance. The Japanese immigrants have been particularly helpful in developing the agricultural resources of the region, especially the production of fruits and vegetables.

In recent decades, entrepreneurs of many origins have tended to come into the Oriente to participate in the program to open up and exploit its resources. These include Bolivians from the Altiplano, Europeans, and North Americans, among others.

The ethnic and racial differences between the people of the Oriente and those of the westerly parts of Bolivia have been a major factor in the traditional feeling of separatism that has characterized the region, particularly the department of Santa Cruz. Another contributor to this feeling, undoubtedly, has been the great physical distance separating the Oriente from the parts of Bolivia in which most of its people have lived and where its government was located.

Secessionist movements have existed in Santa Cruz virtually since the achievement of Bolivian independence. They have from time to time been encouraged by elements in neighboring countries, and in some instances have favored association of Santa Cruz with Argentina and in others with Brazil. However, on other occasions, proponents of separation from Bolivia have sought to establish in the Oriente a completely independent republic.

The construction of a paved highway connecting the Santa Cruz region with the western part of the republic as well as the growth of air travel between the various parts of Bolivia have reduced the isolation of Santa Cruz from the Altiplano and the Yungas. However, the feeling of differentness from the rest of the republic has by no means disappeared in the Santa Cruz region.

EDUCATION AND HEALTH

The level of formal education in Bolivia is still one of the lowest to be found anywhere in Latin America. This reflects the centuries-long division of the country between a very small white or near-white elite, which was more or less well educated, and the Indian masses, who had very little formal education until the Bolivian National Revolution of the 1950s. Since the victory of the revolution in 1952 substantial progress has been made in extending the school system among the Indian peasantry, but the traditional deprivation of the indigenous majority of formal education has only begun to change.

The eleventh edition of the *Encyclopedia Britannica* in 1910 presented a clear view of the traditional state of education in Bolivia at the beginning of the century:

> . . . According to official estimates for 1901, the total number of primary schools in the republic was 733, with 938 teachers and 41,587 pupils. . . . The school enrolment was only one in 43.7 of population, compared with one in 10 for Argentina. The schools are largely under the control of the municipalities, though nearly half of them are maintained by the national government, by the Church and by private means. There were in the same year 13 institutions of secondary and 14 of superior instruction.

Some progress in educational matters was made between the turn of the century and the outbreak of the Bolivian National Revolution in 1952. However, it was not until the revolution that the government deliberately set about to extend educational facilities to the Indian majority of the population. Particularly in the early years of the revolution, the new Ministry of Peasant Affairs made extensive efforts to meet the sudden increase in demand for education by the Indians. However, as time went on, even the enthusiasm of the leaders of the revolution for meeting the Indians' educational needs waned in the face of matters that seemed more pressing.

One of the most impressive immediate results of the 1952 revolution and the establishment of a ministry that the peasants quickly came to regard as their mediator with the government and more generally with the non-Indian society of Bolivia was the enthusiasm of the Indians to educate their children. There were many cases in which the Indians of a particular community built a schoolhouse and then went to the ministry to seek a teacher. The Ministry of Peasant Affairs was pressed to find enough people to meet this demand, and in many cases, the people chosen to be local teachers were Indians who had themselves received little more than a primary school education. Subsequently, the ministry developed programs to try to upgrade such primary teachers.

As a result of these and other programs to develop the Bolivian educational system, there were by the late 1970s some 8,887 primary schools in the republic, with 730,554 students and 30,075 teachers. There were also 383 secondary schools, with 122,124 students and 7,531 teachers, as well as 80 vocational schools with 1,060 teachers and 10,452 students, and teacher training institutions with 314 teachers and 5,896 students.

Bolivia also has a system of higher education. The *Encyclopedia Britannica* at the beginning of the present century took as disparaging a view of it as of the lower levels of education at that time, referring to the "so-called universities at Sucre (Chuquisaca), La Paz, Cochabamba, Tarija, Potosí, Santa Cruz and Oruro—

all of which give instruction in law, the first three in medicine, and the first four in theology. The university at Sucre, which dates from colonial times, and that at La Paz, are the only ones on the list sufficiently well equipped to merit the title."

The Bolivian university system has improved considerably since the early 1900s. As was true in virtually all of Latin America, the Bolivian universities were profoundly influenced by the University Reform, which began in Argentina in 1918. As a result, the universities no longer concentrated only on law, medicine, and theology. Indeed, theology has been eliminated entirely from the state universities, and the physical and social sciences have been introduced in the universities. Continuing attempts have been made since the 1920s to obtain autonomy for the schools of higher learning to run their own affairs.

However, the Bolivian universities are still far from being the best in Latin America. This is the result partly of the poverty of the country because sufficient resources have not been provided to maintain a first-rate system of higher education. And partly it is because of the military role in the government of the country, making succeeding governments particularly suspicious of "subversive" ideas.

A third factor has perhaps been more important than either national poverty or military government in debilitating the Bolivian universities. This has been the extreme politicization of the universities. Both the faculties and student bodies of the Bolivian institutions of higher learning have tended for several decades to be dominated by political groups. Those dissenting from the dominant ideology or political element have tended to be purged from the faculty or the student body.

By the late 1970s, there were eight universities in Bolivia: those of Sucre, Oruro, Potosí, Cochabamba, Santa Cruz, Tarija, Trinidad, and La Paz. In all these there were 37,692 students and 3,026 faculty members.

Obviously, the educational establishment in Bolivia is still inadequate. It was estimated in the late 1970s that only about one-half of the children who were supposedly subject to compulsory education were actually in school and at least 40 percent of the people between 15 and 50 years of age were illiterate.

The quality of education received was also highly questionable. Until 1979, the official language of instruction at all levels of education was Spanish, even though many children and youngsters certainly did not know that language, at least when they began their education. Since 1979, instruction has been officially permitted in Quechua and Aymara.

Health services are at least as inadequate in the later twentieth-century Bolivia as is the educational system. A social security system provides a modicum of medical service to the workers of the mines and many of those of the cities. However, the great majority of the peasants are still largely unserved by hospitals, doctors, nurses, and other medical personnel and services.

The Ministry of Peasant Affairs sought in the early years of the Bolivian

National Revolution to extend health services to the rural parts of the country. A number of primitive medical facilities were established in the rural areas, with practical nurses who could give innoculations, carry out first aid, and facilitate transfer to hospitals of some patients who needed more extensive medical help (if such hospitals were available).

However, these efforts did not by any means provide an adequate level of medical services in Bolivia. In 1972, there were 2,143 doctors in the country, an average of one for every 2,422 persons. There were 9,451 hospital beds, or one per 522 inhabitants. Daily per capita caloric intake was 1,980 calories as compared with the United Nations Food and Agricultural Organization's recommended minimum of 2,480 calories a day.

The health situation was also reflected in the birthrate of 43.7 per 1,000, and deathrate of 18 per 1,000. The life expectancy at birth of a Bolivian in the 1970–75 period was 45.7 years for males and 47.9 years for females, 15 to 20 years or more below the life expectancy in the highly industrialized countries and the better-off developing ones.

RELIGION

Officially, Bolivia is a Roman Catholic country. Indeed, for most of the first hundred years of its independence, Roman Catholicism was not only the official religion, but the only one that could be practiced openly. However, for most of the population of the country, their Catholicism was more apparent than real. The *Encyclopedia Britannica* in 1910 commented that

> The constitution of Bolivia, art. 2, defines the attitude of the republic toward the Church in the following words—'The state recognizes and supports the Roman Apostolic Catholic religion, the public exercise of any other worship being prohibited, except in the colonies, where it is tolerated.' The toleration is tacitly extended to resident foreigners belonging to other religious sects. . . . The domesticated Indians profess the Roman Catholic faith, but it is tinged with superstition of their ancestors.

The constitution has been altered since the early decades of the twentieth century insofar as the status of religion is concerned. The document of 1947, which (with modifications) still remains in effect, recognizes Roman Catholicism as the state religion but provides for free expression of other faiths.

The Catholic Church in Bolivia has a cardinal archbishop with his base in Sucre and another archbishop in La Paz. There are also six dioceses, with their seats in Cochabamba, Santa Cruz, Oruro, Potosí, Riberalta, and Tarija as well as "vicars apostolic" in several other cities.

The relatively weak hold of the church on the country's politics is reflected in the fact that since 1911 all marriages have had to be performed by civil authorities in order to be legally valid. It is also shown by the existence since 1932 of a law permitting divorce.

Regardless of the official status of Catholicism in Bolivia, however, the fact is that the great majority of the people, the Indians, are only superficially Roman Catholics, at best. They still maintain loyalty to the gods of their ancestors. The more than four and a half centuries of missionary work by Catholic priests (and several decades of activity by Protestant groups as well) have not succeeded in establishing Christianity as the real faith of the Bolivian Indians. Even when they ostensibly worship the Christian deity and pay homage to the Catholic saints, more often than not the Christian symbols are little more than a thin veneer for one of the pre-Columbian gods.

The symbiosis of Christianity and the pre-Columbian religions has been reflected on a number of occasions in the past by the growth of millennial religious cults that even inspired revolts against the existing order. The last of these to be recorded took place in 1892 when a prophet who called himself Apiawaiki led a group of Indian followers in revolt, assuring them that the bullets of the government's soldiers were nothing more than water.

The Catholic Church in Bolivia is severely undermanned. In recent decades, it has sought the help of priests from other countries, including Spain as well as the United States and Canada. Even with their help, however, only a small proportion of the rural population has the services of Catholic clergymen.

During the twentieth century, various Protestant missionary groups have worked in Bolivia. Perhaps the most outstanding of these has been the Seventh-day Adventists, who have provided medical missionaries and maintained hospitals and other health facilities for various Indian groups.

LITERATURE AND THE SOCIAL SCIENCES

A combination of poverty, a very limited reading public, and political tyranny has not been particularly conducive to the flourishing of literature and the arts in Bolivia. However, the country has by no means been without development in these fields, particularly since the national catastrophe of the Chaco War and the soul searching that it provoked.

Probably the outstanding literary figure in Bolivia before the Chaco War period was Franz Tamayo. A poet and a self-taught sociologist and anthropologist, he did pioneer work in seeking out the Indian roots of the nation and trying to understand them.

Since the Chaco War, a considerable literature has developed, particularly that of the novel. The writers have been concerned, understandably, with the different groups that make up the people of Bolivia. The rural Indian has been a major subject of Bolivian fiction. Even before the Chaco War, Alcides Arguedas had written and published (as early as 1919) the classic novel *Raza de Bronce* about the indigenous people. Since the war a number of other writers, including José Felipe Costas Arguedas, Raúl Botelho Gosalvez, Max Mendoza, and Natty Pēnaranda de Guillén Pinto, have written fiction around the subject of the Indian peasant. Perhaps Jesús Lara's several novels on this theme are the best known outside of the country.

The miner has also been the subject for Bolivian fiction writers. Among the major works on this subject have been Roberto Leiton's *Los Eternos Vagabundos*, Fernando Ramírez Velarde's *Socavones de Anguiia*, and Augusto Cespedes' *Metal del Diablo*, perhaps the most famous.

The cholos of the cities have likewise been written about in fictional form. Among the more important authors who have dealt with them have been Carlos Medinaceli, Antonio Díaz Villamil, Victor Hugo Villegas, and Federico Avila.

The end of the Chaco War brought a heightened interest in nonfictional studies of the Bolivian reality. José Antonio Arce, politician as well as social scientist, was one of the early figures of note in the field of soicology in the 1940s and 1950s. More recently, the Trotskyist leader Guillermo Lora has written a monumental four-volume history of the Bolivian organized labor movement, a summary version of which has been published in English.

The study of economics is more limited in Bolivia than in many of the other Latin American countries. Until the 1960s, it was greatly hampered by the fact that the teaching of the subject was limited very largely to the perspective of nineteenth-century Marxism. However, in the last two decades, a number of young Bolivians have studied abroad—in Chile, the United States, and elsewhere—and this has resulted both in altering the study of the subject in the country's major universities and in the development of a small corps of economists trained in modern ideas and techniques.

THE ARTS

The fine arts are not as highly developed in contemporary Bolivia as in some of the other Latin American countries. For example, there are few if any spectacular examples of twentieth-century architecture in the republic. However, during the colonial period there existed in Upper Peru several outstanding examples of the so-called "mestizo" architectural style, that is Baroque architecture executed by Indian workmen and perhaps even Indian architects, and reflecting both the inspiration then current in Spain and that which was traditional with the indigenous people of the colony. Two of these buildings were the Jesuit La Compañia church at Potosí, built between 1700 and 1707, and the San Francisco church in La Paz, which was constructed between 1753 and 1772.

However, the Bolivian National Revolution of the 1950s aroused something of the same kind of Indian sentiment there as had appeared in Mexico at the time of its revolution several decades earlier. This found some expression in painting. The revolutionary governments commissioned a number of artists to adorn the walls of various public buildings with mural paintings of the country's ordinary folk in their various activities. Although no outstanding figures such as the Mexican trio of Diego Rivera. José Clemente Orozco, and David Alfaro Siqueiros appeared in Bolivia, some of these murals are of interest. There are also a fair number of Bolivian artists who have devoted their efforts to smaller works, and some of the etchings of Indian scenes and of Indian people are of particular interest.

The country has not been rich enough, or its government has not been willing, to maintain first rank musical organizations. There does exist a National Symphony Orchestra, but it is more amateur than professional.

The most important artistic work of Bolivia is what might be called folk art. Indian craftsmen still produce very fine wood carvings of themselves, llamas, and a variety of other subjects. Elaborate silver jewelry, some of which is of high quality, but which on balance is not as good as that of neighboring Peru, is also crafted by Indian artisans.

As did their ancestors many centuries ago, the Indians still produce very interesting and eyecatching textiles. Although the techniques of producing these have changed and modern chemical dyes now are used in place of those made by the Indians themselves, the textiles of Bolivia are still one of the country's major artistic accomplishments. They are to be seen every day, particularly in the garments of the Indian and cholo women.

CONCLUSION

Bolivia remains to this day a country that is strikingly different from most of the other nations of the hemisphere. Its geography is unique and its people are more thoroughly Indian than are those of any other country in America. Still far from being a single integrated nation, its rural Indian population still lives in comparative isolation from the urban cholos and "whites."

2

THE ECONOMY

Since pre-Columbian times, the majority of the people of Bolivia have been farmers. For over four centuries, mining has provided most of the money income, exports, and government revenue, and has been the source of fabulous fortunes wrested from the forbidding mountains at the cost of the sweat, blood, and oppression of the miners.

In spite of half a millennia of digging treasures out of the mountains of the High Andes and half a century of extracting from oil-rich lands in the Oriente, selling most of these treasures abroad, the Bolivian economy remains backward. A large proportion of the people are still outside the market, transportation facilities continue to be inadequate, productivity is low, the amount of physical capital employed is scanty, and most of the people are abysmally poor.

AGRICULTURE OF THE ALTIPLANO

Most of the Indian peasants, particularly those of the Altiplano, remain principally subsistence farmers. The greater part of their effort is dedicated to growing enough for themselves and their families to eat. They build their own homes and other necessary buildings. Peasant families still make many of their own utensils, tools, and some of the clothes they wear. The surpluses that they sell to obtain necessities from the cities are still marginal and subordinate to what they produce for their own use.

Much of the Altiplano is extremely difficult for agriculture. In large areas of the southern departments of the region, the land is good for little but grazing, and in other parts of that same region not even enough vegetation grows to sustain the sheep, llamas, and other animals. Wind erosion destroys much of the fertility the soil might otherwise have. In those segments of the Altiplano, the Indian communities are widely scattered, existing only where sufficient rainfall or occasional streams originating in the snows of the high mountains have made it possible for the land to support enough vegetation for the Indian to eke out a meager living.

The richest part of the Altiplano is the region within a few score leagues of Lake Titicaca. In this area, there is enough rain, the soil is moist, and the climate is sufficiently salubrious to sustain a comparatively large peasant population. As their ancestors have done for perhaps a thousand years, the Indians have aided nature by terracing substantial areas, building up rich soil behind the stone walls of the terraces.

It is in the Lake Titicaca area, particularly in the department of La Paz, that the Indians grow the country's principal temperate crops. Two of these are of particular importance for the peasants: potatoes and quinoa. In addition, they grow small quantities of wheat and barley and substantial amounts of oca, an indigenous tuber.

The "Irish" potato is a native of the High Andes. It was taken from there by the Spaniards to Europe and was dispersed virtually throughout the globe. The Indians have vast ancestral experience in growing the potato, developing strains that can resist the rigors of altitude and climate. They are quite loathe to experiment with new ways of growing it or with new strains of seed with which they are not familiar.

The potato is a key element in the Indians' diet. As Harold Osborne has explained:

> Both potatoes and ocas are eaten mainly in the dehydrated form known as *chuno* or *tunta*. The tubers are first soaked in water for a week or so and then exposed in the open to the alternate heat of the sun by day and frost by night. After some ten days of this treatment, when they begin to pulp, the remaining moisture is trodden out with the feet and they are left in the open for three or four weeks to dry out. The resulting product is quite hard and dry, about the size of a walnut. . . *chuno* is pleasanter to eat than the unprocessed potato, has the consistency of a cooked chestnut and a distinctive and agreeable flavor. [Pp. 14–15]

The principal grain crop of the Indian peasants of the Altiplano is the native plant quinoa, related to millet. The Indians make a kind of soup out of this grain, and they also distill it to make *chicha*, the indigenous intoxicating beverage.

The Altiplano Indians are herdsmen as well as farmers. Two native animals, the alpaca and the llama, as well as sheep, introduced nearly 500 years ago by the Spaniards, are the principal beasts involved.

The vicuña, alpaca, and llama are three animals native to the Andes, said to have some relationship to the camel family. The vicuña does not breed well in captivity, and is becoming increasingly rare. However, the alpaca and the llama, and particularly the llama, are bred by the Indian farmers.

The llama was for many centuries the principal beast of burden of the High Andes. However, it tends to be a cantankerous beast, seemingly possessing a very strong will. When annoyed at its human master or at a passerby, it "spits" at the offender. When overloaded by its master, it refuses to budge until the load is lightened. However, in spite of—or perhaps because of—this seemingly independent spirit, the llama is of great value to the Indians. It is sure-footed and able to go long distances without drinking and on relatively little food.

The llama and the sheep are both multipurpose animals for the Indians. The llama provides wool as well as transport service; the sheep is the source of lamb and mutton as well as wool. However, the Indians traditionally have had a very conservative attitude towards their sheep and llamas. These flocks have had a great deal more than utilitarian value to owners. They have been symbols of both wealth and prestige among the Indians, and the larger the flock, the more of both the proprietor is presumed to have.

As a result of these traditional attitudes, some Indians tend to be "llama-poor," and "sheep-poor," that is, they have larger numbers of the animals than a purely commercial calculus would advise. Also, the Indians tend to be very cautious about treating their charges in ways that custom does not dictate.

Thus, when the government of President Barrientos sought in the 1960s, with financial aid and technical advice from U.S. aid officials, to help the Indians exploit their flocks more economically, they encountered substantial resistance. Many of the Indians were by no means eager to use the new and more or less modern sheep dips that the government installed in various places in the Altiplano, designed to facilitate the production of a better quality of wool. Even more reluctant were the Indians to accept the idea that they might considerably improve their own economic position if they would select from their herds of sheep some to sell for slaughtering. This idea ran counter, obviously, to the non-economic value the herds had for their masters, whose prestige and wealth seemed imperiled by the idea of purposely thinning out the flocks.

The highland Indian does not breed cattle in any significant numbers. However, he does keep smaller animals, including pigs, goats, and poultry. In 1978 there were said to be 8,460,000 sheep, 3,000,000 goats, 1,350,000 pigs, and 8,200,000 poultry in Bolivia, although the figures available do not indicate what proportion of these were located in the Altiplano.

Most of the vegetable and animal products grown by the Altiplano Indians are raised principally for their own use, as indicated. When the lands around Lake Titicaca were in the hands of large private landowners before the 1952 revolution, substantial quantities of grains and other products were grown by the Indians on the landlords' instructions for sale in the cities and towns. At the same time, on plots assigned to them for their own use, the Indians grew crops and animals on a subsistence basis.

Since the agrarian reform of the 1950s, there has been considerable controversy concerning whether or not land redistribution resulted in a diminution of actual production by the new Indian peasant landowners. What is certain is that smaller surpluses were available for sale to the urban centers. However, it seems likely that much of what had formerly been produced for sale was now being consumed by the peasants and their families. This was attested to by the fact that the average weight of Indian army draftees was substantially higher a decade or so after the agrarian reform than it had been before 1952.

The idea of farming principally to grow products for sale has spread only slowly. Although the advantages of possessing such things as bicycles and transistor radios, which can be purchased with cash earned by selling the products of their labor, have been becoming increasingly evident to the highland Indians, they have remained quite conservative. As a group, they have been quite unwilling to shift over to production principally for the market rather than for themselves.

They have also been equally hesitant about experimenting with new ways of farming. While not sure of the new dangers the adoption of new methods of cultivation might entail yet very much aware of the catastrophic results to themselves and their families that might result from the failure of crops, the Indians have continued to move very cautiously in modernizing their agricultural processes.

The natural conservatism of the Indians in this regard has been reinforced by the fact that few if any governments since the land redistribution took effect in the 1950s have seen fit to invest any substantial sums in trying to develop and teach the farmers new methods and new techniques. There has never been developed any extensive agricultural experimental system, not to mention any extension system to tell the farmers about and demonstrate new methods of farming that have been proven effective, although a beginning has been made with such services in the Lake Titicaca area.

Other elements of agricultural infrastructure have also not been developed to any degree in the Altiplano or Yungas areas. Credit for financing the crops of the Indian peasants or for long-run improvements in their holdings has been sparse, when not nonexistent. Little has been done by the governmental authorities to develop facilities for marketing the peasants' produce or to warehouse it.

Hence, the process of modernizing the Altiplano Indian agriculture has been left largely to the Indians themselves, and to small-scale entrepreneurs, more often than not ex-peasants themselves, with a little more innovative spirit and financial resources than the great mass of their fellows. In a widespread new phenomenon since the revolution, the owner of a truck (or a few of them) buys up the Indians' surpluses at harvest time and transports them to the cities. These entrepreneurs have, understandably, followed the policy of buying cheap and selling dear, to the disadvantage of the Indian farmer. Sometimes they are small-scale moneylenders as well as transporters of products.

AGRICULTURE OF THE YUNGAS

The area of the Yungas, the valleys between the Altiplano and the lowlands of the Oriente, is one of the major centers of Bolivian agriculture. Of particular importance are the valleys to the east of the city of La Paz and those in the vicinity of Cochabamba, Sucre, and Tarija.

As in the Altiplano, the majority of the rural population of the Yungas region consists of Indians. However, in parts of the area, particularly in the Cochabamba Valley, the peasants have been more nearly assimilated into cholo status and have been more closely involved in national political life before and since the Bolivian National Revolution of the 1950s than has been the case with most rural Altiplano Indians.

Before the revolution, large landholdings were prevalent in much of the Yungas area, most notably in the Valley of Cochabamba. In fact, the Nationalist Revolutionary Movement government chose Ucureña, not far from the city of Cochabamba, as the place for the official signing of the Agrarian Reform Law. Since the agrarian reform, the small peasant proprietor has been the typical farmer of that part of Bolivia, as in the Altiplano.

The conditions for agriculture in the Yungas region are very different from those in the Altiplano. For one thing, there is a great deal more rainfall in the Yungas than in the highlands. And the lower altitude of the valley areas means that most of the crops grown there are those characteristic of semitropical latitudes, rather than the temperate-type products grown in the Altiplano. Finally, the valleys do not lend themselves to the grazing of sheep and other domesticated animals as in the Altiplano.

Among the major crops of the Yungas area are coffee, cacao, bananas, and sugarcane. Unlike the situation in the highlands, these products are not grown principally for the consumption of the peasants who cultivate them, but rather for sale commercially. For the most part, they are transported to the urban centers of the Yungas and to the cities of the Altiplano, particularly La Paz.

COCA TRADE

Since pre-Columbian times, the coca plant has been one of the major crops grown in the Yungas area of Bolivia. It derives its name from the Quechua word *kuka*. It undoubtedly had certain sacred significance in the indigenous religious cults.

Traditionally, the Indians have chewed the dried leaves of the coca plant. It acts as a stimulant, and is variously credited with helping the Indians resist the effects of high altitudes and the extremely cold weather of the high Andes. On the other hand, there have been some observers who have argued that the chewing of coca has been largely responsible for the alleged lassitude and passivity of the highland Indians of Bolivia and neighboring countries. The use of the coca leaf in Bolivia is not confined to the Indians. Even a stranger visiting the country is likely to be offered a mild tea made from the leaf as a protection against the effects of the high altitude and scarce oxygen.

The uses of the coca leaf are not confined to helping natives and visitors bear more easily the rigors of the altitude and climate of the Bolivian Altiplano. On the contrary, the leaf is the raw material out of which the drug cocaine is made. With the dramatic growth of the international drug trade, and particularly the commerce in cocaine in recent years, the whole character of coca agriculture in the Bolivian Yungas has altered dramatically.

Until the 1970s, the cultivation and commercialization of the coca leaf was largely a Bolivian domestic activity. However, it has since become a gigantic international trade that is no longer in the hands of small-time businessmen, but rather is controlled and managed by the same people who control the military forces and the government of Bolivia.

As the international demand—particularly in the United States—for cocaine increased, the possibility of converting the modest cultivation of the coca plant for the limited Bolivian market into a major part of the international drug market boomed. From a business in the hands of small-time Indian and cholo dealers, it came to be one dominated by top officers in the Bolivian armed forces.

With the seizure of power in 1980 by General Luis García Meza, the country's drug smugglers took over the government of Bolivia. By the middle of 1981 there were reported to be three major groups involved in the smuggling of Bolivian cocaine out of the country, ultimately to the United States and Europe. One of these rings was reported to be headed by a member of the president's cabinet and another by the commander of one of the branches of Bolivia's three armed forces.

This rapid growth of the illegal (but officially sponsored) drug trade dramatically altered the country's balance of payments situation. It was reported that by 1981, income from the cocaine trade was bringing in between $1.2 billion and $1.5 billion a year. This compared with the $373,710,000 in 1978 from the sale of tin, officially the country's largest export.

There is little doubt about the fact that the distribution of the income from this illegal cocaine trade has been exceedingly unequal. Although the Indians who grow the drug have certainly profited modestly from the increased demand for their product, the great bulk of the profits have gone to the entrepreneurs in the military and their collaborators who have been principally responsible for organizing the export of the product.

It is too early to know what the long-run effects of the cocaine trade will be. Almost certainly, the peasants of the Yungas have been stimulated to shift from production of other products to the growing of coca. Whether such a shift will have a lasting impact on reducing the ability of the Yungas area to provide the foodstuffs that it has traditionally sold to the country's urban centers remains to be seen.

AGRICULTURE OF THE ORIENTE

One of the major long-term accomplishments of the Bolivian National Revolution has been the stimulation of the economic development of the eastern part of the country, the Oriente. Agriculture and those industries that are based on the processing of agricultural products have benefited most from this economic development.

The economy of the Oriente must logically be divided between the northern part of the area and its southern region. It has been the southern part, and especially the department of Santa Cruz, that has benefited principally from the economic development efforts of the last three decades.

In the northern departments of Pando and Beni there have traditionally been two types of economic activity: rubber production and cattle raising. Bolivia was for several decades a major participant in the rubber boom that began in the last quarter of the nineteenth century. However, the area in which the rubber trees were located was very difficult to reach from the Altiplano, and the processed rubber was shipped down the Bolivian rivers to the Amazon and ultimately out through the Brazilian port of Belem. The rubber boom had another disadvantage for Bolivia. Most of the people who swarmed into the area to collect the latex were from Brazil and they ultimately revolted against Bolivian authority. In 1903 Bolivia recognized the cession of the largest part of its rubber-producing region, Acre, to Brazil by the Treaty of Petropolis. In the region that remained Bolivian, small quantities of rubber still continued to be gathered. However, rubber was no longer a major Bolivian export. In 1974, rubber exports from Bolivia were valued at only $1.9 million.

During the twentieth century the principal source of income arising from the northern part of the Oriente has been cattle. Two departments, those of Beni and Santa Cruz, contain most of the country's cattle herds. In 1978, it was reported that there were 3.8 million head of cattle in Bolivia.

Although much of the territory of the department of Beni is forested, there are sizable plains areas. Some of these are subject to periodic flooding, but it is in these plains that the great majority of the cattle of the region are bred, as they have been for four centuries. Reportedly, it was Spanish monks who first introduced European cattle into the region early in the colonial period.

Some of the cattle of this region of the Oriente are exported to Brazil and Peru. However, the largest commercial amount goes to other parts of Bolivia. Until recent decades, it was very difficult to get meat from the Beni to markets in the cities of the highlands. However, during the last few decades there has developed a lively beef trade by air from the east to the Altiplano. Beef, although more costly than meats originating in the highlands, is readily available in the major cities.

Grazing and agriculture have both expanded in the Beni area since the Bolivian National Revolution of the 1950s. However, the greatest impact of the economic development policies of the revolutionary government has been felt in the department of Santa Cruz. The center of that region is the city of Santa Cruz. Some idea of the effect of the economic development of the region in recent decades can be gotten from the changes that have occurred in that city.

John A. Crow described the town of Santa Cruz when he visited it in 1942:

> The general impression was of a squalid cluster of mud houses in the middle of nowhere whose sole connection with the outside world was the airplane. . . . The town radiated like a squat and filthy line of barnyards from that central axis. Pigs and chickens scrounged in the dirt streets, and the smell of outdoor toilet facilities permeated the air. [P. 773]

Forty years later, Santa Cruz was the second largest city of Bolivia, outpaced only by La Paz. Its population had grown to an estimated 125,000 by the end of the 1960s and 237,128 by 1976. It was by far the most rapidly growing of all the country's urban centers. Modern buildings had replaced most of the mud huts described by Crow, and the city had expanded far beyond its former limits. It was one of the principal transportation centers of the continent, with railway connections to Brazil and Argentina, and a major highway to Cochabamba and from there to the Altiplano.

The expansion of agriculture in its environs has been one of the principal reasons for the growth of the city of Santa Cruz. The MNR party government of the 1952-64 period began the policies of encouraging mass migration to the area between Cochabamba and Santa Cruz and of helping to finance the development of commercial agriculture in the Santa Cruz area. These policies have been continued by the military regimes that came after the overthrow of the MNR.

Along the Cochabamba—Santa Cruz Highway and roads branching out from it, the Indian settlers have in many cases continued to be subsistence farmers, producing only small surpluses for the market. However, to the east, north, and south of the city of Santa Cruz, commercial agriculture has been predominant, principally in the production of tropical crops. These include particularly sugar, rice, cotton, citrus fruits, and coffee. Between 1971 and 1975, the output of sugar and rice quadrupled, and by 1978 the country produced 3,246,621 tons of sugar, 88,580 tons of rice, and 17,335 tons of cotton lint. (For purposes of comparison, a normal Cuban sugar crop runs from 5 to 6 million tons.) The country is self-sufficient in these products, and exports some sugar and rice to neighboring nations.

The large commercial agricultural enterprises have received considerable help from the government. The Banco Agricola has extended considerable credit, which they have also been able to obtain from private banking firms. In addition, much of the limited expenditure by successive governments on agricultural research and extension services has been made available to these large enterprises.

The commercial agriculture of the Oriente is modernized. This is demonstrated by the fact that whereas in the Altiplano some 90 percent of all the energy used in agriculture is that of animals, in the Oriente 90 percent of the energy is provided by machines.

THE MINING INDUSTRY

Since soon after the arrival of the Spaniards in the sixteenth century, mining has provided most of the exports of Bolivia. Although the minerals that are exported have changed, their importance to the economy has altered very little. In the late 1970s, the mines provided 11 percent of the gross national product, 25 percent of the revenues of the government, and 75 percent of the foreign exchange earned by the Bolivian economy. However, they employed only about 3 percent of the labor force.

In the last decades of the nineteenth century, tin passed silver as Bolivia's principal mineral product. A century later, tin is still the most important mineral of the Bolivian mountains, although its relative importance has been declining and its future is somewhat problematical. Bolivia is still the second largest world producer of tin.

The development of the tin industry was completely in the hands of private firms, and by the late 1920s tin mining was dominated by three enterprises, those of Patiño, Aramayo, and Hochschild. These companies were incorporated abroad and had considerable foreign capital invested in them.

However, since 1952 the dominant firm in the tin-mining industry has been the government-owned Corporación Minera de Bolivia (COMIBOL). Since its inception, it has been plagued with a wide variety of problems: overbureaucratization of management, inefficient use of personnel, almost constant labor-management problems, inadequate transport facilities, and government control of the foreign exchange that it earned. Even more significant in the long run has been the fact that COMIBOL has been working mines that had to a considerable degree been worked out before the firm came into existence. Although it is the only company authorized to explore for new mineral veins, it has spent very little on doing so since 1952, in part because the system of taxation on the firm tends to discourage such expenditures.

In the early 1960s the government of President Víctor Paz Estenssoro launched a program to reorganize COMIBOL, the so-called Triangular Plan. It was continued by the governments that succeeded the MNR regime, but was only partially successful in rationalizing the firm's operations and making them more efficient.

Since the 1960s, there has been considerable expansion of so-called "medium" mining firms. These are privately owned enterprises, and they have engaged in substantial investments in expanding and modernizing their operations. They are generally recognized to be more efficient than COMIBOL, and their share of the total output of tin and other minerals has been expanding slowly but steadily. By the 1970s, they had been successful enough so that their political influence had become of substantial significance and they were widely credited with being the major political element supporting the generally unpopular devaluation of the Bolivian currency by the Banzer government in 1973.

Until 1970, all of Bolivia's tin was exported in the form of concentrates. However, the government of President Alfredo Ovando (1969–70) began the construction of a refinery, which was completed a few years later. As a consequence, by 1978 about 40 percent of the tin exports were refined.

By the late 1970s, tin still represented about one-half of all of the minerals exported. On the average the ore being mined contained only 3.5 percent tin. Production of tin in 1978 amounted to 30,880 tons, which accounted for $373,710,000 out of a total value of Bolivian exports of $640,300,000.

At least since World War I, Bolivia's tin industry has been faced with erratic price behavior in the international market. During the 1920s, the International Tin Cartel was organized by the major tin-producing countries, but it was not able to deal very effectively with the crisis that the Great Depression brought to the industry. After World War II, the cartel, which still existed, had some success in bringing relative stability to the market.

Yet another major factor has influenced the international price situation. This has been the stockpiling policies of the United States government since World War II. Sometimes, U.S. action has helped to keep up the price, but on various occasions decisions by the United States to reduce its stockpiles have brought substantial price declines and have provoked strong protests from the government of Bolivia.

The future of the tin-mining industry probably depends more than anything else on the discovery of new veins of the ore. Many experts agree that there are substantial additional reserves that have not been discovered. By the late 1970s, less than 2 percent of Bolivian land was said to have been explored for minerals.

New and richer sources of tin would undoubtedly result in much less costly output of the mineral. However, in order to find and open up such reserves, very large capital expenditures would be necessary. So far, no significant moves have been taken to undertake any such expansion program.

In addition to tin, a number of other minerals are produced in and exported from Bolivia. Several of these are mined jointly with tin, and they include silver, antimony, tungsten, lead, copper, zinc, bismuth, wolfram, and cadmium.

Two minerals are found principally in the Oriente. One is alluvial gold, found in the Alto Beni, and exploited principally by miners' cooperatives. Some 770 kilograms were exported in 1978. The other is the very large reserves of iron ore which are found near the Brazilian border city of Corumbá. The full exploitation of this iron ore has not yet begun. However, in time it may provide not only another major export, but also the basis for substantial industrial development in the eastern part of the republic.

PETROLEUM

Petroleum has brought Bolivia hope, disappointment, and disaster. Oil does exist in the Oriente and it has been modestly exploited. However, expectation that petroleum would surpass tin as the major export and that the country would experience a bonanza similar to Venezuela, Ecuador, and the Arab countries of the Middle East has been frustrated. Greed over petroleum was certainly one of the factors provoking the disastrous Chaco War with Paraguay in the 1930s.

By the outbreak of the Chaco conflict, the Standard Oil Company of New Jersey had begun the exploitation of Bolivian oil reserves in the Santa Cruz area. However, Bolivia had not by that time become a major producer, and most of the oil from the Santa Cruz field was used internally, although small quantities were exported.

Since the first development of petroleum in Bolivia, the government's policies toward that segment of the economy have changed a number of times. These frequent alterations of policy have undoubtedly had a negative impact on the development of an oil industry.

Before the Chaco War, the aristocratic governments of the "Rosca" depended upon foreign firms, and particularly Standard Oil of New Jersey, to develop the country's oil resources. However, the first post-Chaco War regime of Colonel David Toro expropriated the concessions of Standard Oil in 1936. After long negotiations, a settlement was reached in the early 1940s among the company, the Bolivian government, and the government of the United States concerning the payment to Standard Oil.

Colonel Toro's regime established the Yacimientos Petroliferos Fiscales Bolivianos (YPFB) to take over the former holdings of Standard Oil and to have a monopoly of the petroleum industry in Bolivia. It continued to control the exploration, exploitation, and refining of oil for about two decades.

The YPFB did not prove to be exceedingly efficient. Two decades after its establishment, it was not exporting any petroleum nor able to supply all of the oil products that Bolivia itself needed.

During the first two years of the revolutionary government of President Víctor Paz Estenssoro, substantial resources were invested in the YPFB to provide new machinery and equipment, with the result that the government firm quickly became able to provide virtually all of the country's oil requirements. Subsequently, the Paz Estenssoro government enacted a new law that provided for the possibility of granting new concessions to foreign oil companies.

As a result of the new oil law, various foreign enterprises received concessions to search for new petroleum resources in the late 1950s and early 1960s. The only firm that was clearly successful was Gulf Oil Company of the United States. It not only discovered new oil fields in the Santa Cruz area, but was commissioned by the revolutionary government to build an oil pipeline from the petroleum fields in the Oriente to the Altiplano, and from there to the Chilean Pacific port of Arica. By the 1960s, Bolivia was exporting modest quantities of oil through this pipeline. However, Bolivia did not join the Organization of Petroleum Exporting Countries (OPEC).

In 1969, the military regime of General Alfredo Ovando enacted a new decree-law expropriating the concessions of Gulf Oil, agreeing, however, to compensate the firm for the property that had been seized. The expropriated properties were transferred to the YPFB. In reprisal, Gulf Oil organized a boycott of sale of Bolivian oil outside the country.

Another change in government oil policy took place in the early 1970s. The government of Colonel Hugo Banzer enacted a new decree-law that again authorized the participation of foreign firms in the exploitation of Bolivia's petroleum resources. However, since its enactment, the principal discoveries of the foreign oil companies taking advantage of this law have been in the field of natural gas rather than petroleum.

Bolivia is now self-sufficient in petroleum. All Bolivian oil that is refined in the country is processed by the YPFB. However, Bolivia also exports modest amounts of oil through the pipeline to the Chilean coast. But much more significant is the quantity of natural gas that is exported from the Santa Cruz fields to Argentina, and is soon to be exported also to Brazil. In 1978, crude oil production amounted to 1.87 million cubic meters, and natural gas output was 1,942 million cubic meters.

THE MANUFACTURING SECTOR

The manufacturing sector is a relatively modest part of the Bolivian economy comprised of an artisan portion and another of more or less modern factories. In the late 1970s, only about one-tenth of the total work force was employed in the whole manufacturing sector. Almost two-thirds of the country's industrial workers were employed in La Paz.

Most of Bolivian industries are of two types: processors of the country's raw materials and producers of goods for the ultimate consumer. The raw material processing enterprises include an antimony smelter as well as tin, zinc, bismuth, and tungsten refineries. Also included are oil refineries in Santa Cruz and Cochabamba, and small petrochemical plants. In this same category are sugar refineries in the Santa Cruz regime and enterprises that process rice, cotton, and other agricultural products.

La Paz is the principal center of manufacturing enterprises that produce goods for consumption within the country. There and in other principal cities exist still considerable numbers of small artisan firms that produce clothing, shoes, and a variety of food products.

However, there also exist in La Paz, and to a lesser degree in other cities, more or less modern factories producing consumer goods. The most important of these are certainly textile and clothing plants, which provide much of the national demand for these products by lower income elements of the population.

As a result of its membership in the Andean Group, Bolivia has received allocations of industries within the metal mechanical group, petrochemicals, and the auto parts group. If these concessions are adequately exploited, Bolivian firms will provide these products not only to the national market, but to all of the countries in the Andean Bloc. However, by the early 1980s, very little progress had in fact been made in establishing these industries.

THE TRANSPORT SECTOR

Until the latter part of the nineteenth century, the only way of entering and leaving Bolivia and of transporting goods within the country was by trails passable only to mules or other animals. However, during the last 100 years, railway and road systems and airline routes have been developed that have tied the country more closely to the rest of the world and have brought parts of Bolivia more closely together.

By the mid-1970s, Bolivia had 3,579 kilometers of railroad trackage. Most of this was administered by the State Railway Authority. However, the short line between La Paz and the Lake Titicaca port of Guaqui was still in the hands of a private company and the 500-kilometer spur from Santa Cruz to Yacuiba on the Argentine frontier was run by a joint Bolivian-Argentine mixed commission.

The railroad system connected the capital city of La Paz with the Chilean ports of Antofagasta and Arica. It also provided connections between the capital and the major cities of Oruro, Uyuni, Sucre, and Cochabamba.

Although the railroad system was built for the most part during the half century after the end of the War of the Pacific in the early 1880s, the country's highway network has been of more recent construction. It was particularly stimulated by the Bolivian National Revolution of the 1950s. By 1977 this network extended 37,708 kilometers and included the 497-kilometer Cochabamba-

Santa Cruz Highway, a metaled road from La Paz to Oruro, and unpaved roads from La Paz to Guaqui and Oruro, and from there to Potosí, Tarija, and Bermejo, with branches to Cochabamba, Sucre, and Camiri.

In 1977 there were 86,026 registered motor vehicles in Bolivia. These included 23,000 passenger cars, 22,760 trucks, 5,019 buses, and 6,620 official vehicles of various kinds.

The land transport facilities are supplemented by an extensive network of air routes. The government's firm, Lloyd Aerea Boliviana, provides all of the internal air service, and in 1978 it flew 20,620 hours and carried 1,060,044 passengers. It also offers regular services between La Paz and Lima, São Paulo, Buenos Aires, Miami, Caracas, Salta (Argentina), and Arica. In addition, international air transport is provided to Bolivia by Braniff, Lufthansa, Aerolineas Argentinas, Cruzeiro, Aero Peru, LAN Chile, and Avianca, the Colombian national airline.

BALANCE OF PAYMENTS

The international economic position of Bolivia remains very vulnerable. The country is highly dependent upon the export of a relatively small number of basic commodities, the demand for which tends to vary frequently and erratically. On the other hand, the nation's imports tend to be relatively inelastic, with a propensity toward a steady increase in volume and value.

Tin and other metals are the largest component of Bolivia's exports. Together with petroleum, they constituted in the late 1970s about two-thirds of the total value of goods shipped to the rest of the world. Natural gas and agricultural products from the Oriente have been of growing importance in recent years. Manufactured products make up only about 10 percent of the country's total exports.

The pattern of imports is quite extensive. Among the principal goods brought in from abroad in recent decades have been lard, flour, cooking oil, iron and steel products, mining machinery, pharmaceuticals, paper products, and textiles.

Since the late 1960s, Bolivia has belonged to the Andean Bloc, the other members of which are Peru, Ecuador, Colombia, and Venezuela. The bloc constitutes a common market, which ultimately will have no trade barriers among its members and will have a common protective barrier to the outside world. However, Bolivia, economically one of the weaker members of the group, has special dispensations for maintaining its protection against imports from its partners for a number of years. In spite of these special provisions, there is considerable fear among Bolivian businessmen, and particularly the country's industrialists, that the Andean Group may have a negative impact on the national economy when it goes fully into effect.

Bolivia's balance of payments varies substantially from one year to another, depending upon the current demand for its principal exports. However, more often than not, the country has a favorable balance of trade—that is, of commodities—but has a strongly unfavorable balance of services. These include repayments on its substantial international debt, transport services, and other items. The deficits in this part of the balance of payments have traditionally been met by commercial credit, private bank loans, and foreign aid.

The major change in Bolivia's foreign trade pattern in recent decades has been an alteration in its major trading partners. Until the 1960s, most of Bolivia's trade was with the European Economic Community and the United States. However, since then trade with Brazil and Argentina has increased considerably and that with Bolivia's fellow members of the Andean Group somewhat more modestly. There has also been appreciable growth in trade with Asian countries, including South Korea, Taiwan, Hong Kong, and even with mainland China.

Because of its landlocked situation, Bolivia has to conduct its foreign trade through ports belonging to its neighbors. Its exports and imports go through the Chilean ports of Antofagasta and Arica on the Pacific coast, down the Paraná and Paraguay Rivers (in accordance with an agreement with Paraguay in 1938 and with Argentina in 1976), and via the Brazilian ports of Belem and Santos, in conformity with an accord with Brazil in 1974.

OTHER ATTRIBUTES OF THE ECONOMY

The relatively underdeveloped nature of the Bolivian economy is reflected not only in its agriculture, manufacturing, and foreign trade, but also in various other sectors. Thus, electrical consumption is quite limited, although one of the major economic programs of the government since the Bolivian National Revolution has been the expansion of hydroelectric facilities. In 1978, there was an installed capacity of 428,595 kilowatts throughout the nation. Electrical consumption in that same year was 951,273 mwh.

Other public utilities are also of limited extent. Thus, in 1978, there were only 101,500 telephones in service throughout the country, and they were available only in La Paz, Cochabamba, Oruro, Sucre, Potosí, Santa Cruz, Tarija, Camiri, Tupiza, Villazón, Riberalta, and Trinidad.

The banking system also reflected this same phenomenon. It consisted of several government institutions and a variety of commercial banks, a large proportion of which were foreign owned. The Bolivian national banking system is capped by the Central Bank (Banco Central), which was first established in 1911 as the Banco de la Nación Boliviana, was reorganized in 1928, and nationalized by the government of President Germán Busch in 1939. It fulfills the normal functions of a central bank, emitting the country's legal tender currency, serving as the government's bank, and controlling (to a greater or less degree) the operations of the country's other banks.

There are several other government lending institutions in addition to the Central Bank. The most important are the Banco Minero, which finances the operations of private mining companies, including the purchases abroad of inputs they require and the selling of their output; and the Banco Agricola, which operates in the agricultural field, particularly financing the country's commercial farmers.

Regular commercial banking is handled by a wide variety of different institutions. These include not only a number of domestically owned banks, but also firms with their headquarters abroad, including Argentina, Brazil, and Peru.

The relatively underdeveloped nature of the Bolivian economy is also reflected in a number of other factors. The gross domestic product in 1976 was only $640 per capita. Of the total economically active population of 1,480,000 in 1970, one million workers were involved in agriculture. Some 118,300 were employed in manufacturing, 35,100 in construction, 74,000 in commerce and finance, 65,000 in the employ of the government, 47,800 in mining, and 41,100 in transportation.

CONCLUSION

Bolivia continues to have an underdeveloped economy. Its resources are still largely untapped, and to a large degree are not yet really known. Most of its population is still engaged in agriculture and the majority are still subsistence farmers. Agriculture and mining continue to be the cornerstones of the economy, while manufacturing is only in its infancy. Transport facilities are still relatively primitive and communications are rudimentary. Productivity in agriculture, mining, and most other sectors of the economy continues to be low. The economy still remains excessively dependent upon a very narrow range of primary products exports.

Overall, the economy reflects the fact that the people of Bolivia are still engaged in the process of forming a modern nation. However, the Bolivian National Revolution that started on April 9, 1952, by giving the Indian majority of the population a stake in the nation and by fostering a program of economic development, particularly in the Oriente, gave major impetus to this process of nation building. A generation has passed since then, and at least that much more time must pass before Bolivia will have an integrated economy and a unified nation.

3

PRE-COLUMBIAN
AND COLONIAL BOLIVIA

Before the coming of the Europeans, Bolivia was part of the Inca Empire, ruled from the nearby city of Cuzco, in the south of present-day Peru. The Indians of the Altiplano had had a high level of civilization for many hundreds of years. In the lowland areas to the south and east many of the indigenous people were still primitive hunters and gatherers.

TIAHUANACO

A few miles south of Lake Titicaca there still exist the remains of the city of Tiahuanaco, which almost certainly was the first great center of population, culture, and conquest of this part of the Andean region. The Tiahuanaco civilization is estimated to have existed from about the period A.D. 600 to A.D. 1000, after which it merged into or was conquered by the Inca Empire and culture.

The excavated ruins of Tiahuanaco are undoubtedly only a small part of what was originally there. However, they are sufficient to bear witness to the organizational ability, wealth, and architectural capacity of those who dominated the Tiahuanacan civilization, which is thought to have extended throughout most of the central Andean highland region. As John Crow has observed, the masters of Tiahuanaco "organized government, agriculture, and conquest on a scale vaster than the grandest dreams of all who preceded them on the American scene. . . ." Crow has described the construction at Tiahuanaco and how it was built:

... The massive retaining walls of Tiahuanaco lifted upward by some incomprehensible prodigy of effort and held in place with the aid of metal clamps, formed one of the most gigantic monuments of all time. The Tiahuanacans, like the other American races, never knew the use of the wheel and must have depended almost entirely on human labor to drag these great blocks from the quarries to the final building sites. They probably utilized a combination of crude fiber ropes with which they bound and pulled stones forward while levers were inserted under them from behind to apply force from that direction, and logs or cylindrical rocks over which they might roll were placed underneath. Time was of no concern to the leaders of these people. Whether it took five or fifty years to transport a great building stone was of only the slightest concern. Human labor, too, was a factor which they might extend, stretch, and multiply almost indefinitely. Ten or twenty thousand strong pairs of arms and legs stretched out over a period of one- or twoscore years is the rough equivalent of any machine devised by the ingenious brain of man. [P. 25]

Obviously, an elite group that could order and supervise construction of such edifices by these methods must have ruled over a substantial population. Most of that population was certainly employed in an agricultural economy that provided the surpluses of manpower and sustenance necessary to undertake such tremendous projects.

It is not known for sure, but it is surmised that the Aymara-speaking Indians of Bolivia are the descendants of the Tiahuanacan civilization.

THE INCA CIVILIZATION

By about A. D. 1100 most of present-day Bolivia had passed under the rule of the Incas. They had probably originated somewhere in the vicinity of Lake Titicaca and established their principal center in Cuzco, now a day's slow train ride north of the lake. From there the Incas extended their rule in every direction, not only over Bolivia, but most of present-day Peru and Ecuador, and the southern part of Colombia, northern Chile, and into the northernmost parts of what is today Argentina. At the time of the coming of the Spaniards early in the sixteenth century, the Inca Empire spread over about half a million square miles and controlled between 5 and 6 million people.

Under the Incas, the society of Bolivia was organized much as elsewhere in the empire. The core of the society was the *ayllu*, or community, in theory at least made up of people who had a common ancestor. It was the ayllu that organized and conducted the local economy and served as the base for the empire itself.

The land in each ayllu was divided into three parts, which legally belonged to the Inca, the sun-god (the primary deity of the Inca civilization), and the ayllu. The ayllu's own land was divided among the heads of the families who made up the community, each family receiving about two acres for each male in the family and one acre for each female. Each year, the land of the ayllu was redistributed to take account of demographic changes that had transpired in the previous 12 months.

The land was thus held in common by the ayllu and the plots that each family had the right to use could not be bought, sold, or rented. There were other parts of the ayllu holdings that were farmed cooperatively by all of the members of the community.

Cultivation of the land was strictly regulated. First, all members of the ayllu worked on that part devoted to the sun-god. Then they labored jointly on the holdings of widows and orphans and those members of the community who were too aged or infirm to work their own plots. Only after these tasks had been accomplished were the families of the ayllu free to work on their own small holdings. Finally, all of the members of the community came out to work on the land of the Inca, an activity which was surrounded with considerable celebration and festivity.

In each community there were either two or three warehouses. One held surpluses of good years to carry the community through leaner years. Another stored goods for the sun-god, and a third for those destined for the Inca. These warehouses contained not only food, but also clothing and other goods made by the community members. It is said that the warehouses had enough supplies to meet the needs of the community for several years.

The goods placed in the warehouses of the sun-god and the Inca were at the disposal of the ecclesiastical and political authorities. They were used for the maintenance of the ruling caste, and to supply the warehouses located every 10 to 12 miles along the imperial highways for the use of messengers and soldiers traveling on the Inca's business.

Another major economic activity was grazing. However, the large flocks of llamas and alpacas were the property of the sun-god and the Inca. There were shepherds who moved them from one grazing ground to another, depending upon the season. The work of shearing the animals was done communally by members of the various ayllus, and the wool was placed in common warehouses. From there it was distributed to the women of the various communities, whose task it was to make it into textiles and clothing. This work was carefully supervised by inspectors representing the Inca to assure that it was done and the quality of the products was up to specifications. The textile products turned out by the Peruvian and Bolivian Indians were extraordinarily fine in design and weave.

This society was ruled over by an elite who were jointly known as the Incas. The Inca, the head of the state and the society, usually married his eldest sister (reminiscent of ancient Egypt), but in most cases the ruler also had many concubines and all male descendants of the Inca, whether their mothers were legitimate spouses or concubines, became members of the ruling group of Incas.

It was this ruling caste that provided most of the political and military as well as ecclesiastical leadership of the Inca society. The chief priest was at any given time a close relative—probably a brother or uncle—of the ruling Inca. Most top officials of the state, the priesthood, or the military establishment were also members of the very extended family of the ruling chieftan.

Members of the ruling elite also undoubtedly planned and supervised the very extensive construction projects that were carried out under the Incas. Aside from magnificent buildings in Cuzco and other urban centers, the Incas had constructed a network of roads running from one end of the empire to the other. It was along these roads—which even today provide the base for some of the highways in the countries that were once under Inca rule—that the members of the royal messenger service ran, the conquering armies marched, and the garrisons of the Inca rulers were stationed. Workers were recruited from the various communities of the empire to labor on these public works projects. The knowledge of the highly trained artisans in metals, stone carving, and other arts and crafts was passed from father to son.

During the period of Inca rule in Bolivia it is probable that substantial numbers of people speaking Quechua (the Inca language) were settled in that part of the High Andes, since it was the Inca custom to colonize areas they had conquered. In addition, it may well be that many of the people conquered by the Incas came to speak the language of their conquerors. In any case, the Quechua-speaking people made up the second large group among the Indians of present-day Bolivia.

THE SPANISH CONQUEST

In 1532 a small group of Spaniards led by Francisco Pizarro landed on the coast of Peru and began the process of conquering the Inca Empire. By 1539, Gonzalo Pizarro, one of Francisco's several brothers, led his forces south of Lake Titicaca, established Spanish control over the Bolivian Altiplano, and established the first of the Spanish cities of the region, Chuquisaca, the present-day Sucre.

Most of the first two decades of the conquest of Peru was taken up with civil strife among the conquistadores. The Pizarro brothers, in particular, sought to resist the authority of men sent from Spain to govern over the newly acquired dominions of the king. It was not until the end of these struggles that Bolivia, along with the rest of the ex-Inca Empire, was systematically organized and governed by the Spanish authorities.

It was only in 1563 that Bolivia was established as part of the Audiencia of Charcas, later known as Upper Peru. The jurisdiction of this subdivision of the viceroyalty of Peru was not only present-day Bolivia, but also Paraguay, Argentina, Uruguay, and segments of Peru, Brazil, and Chile as well.

The Bolivian Oriente, in contrast to the Altiplano, was first conquered and settled not by Spaniards coming down from the Altiplano, but by Spanish soldiers coming from Asunción, the capital of present-day Paraguay. Under Ñuflo de Chávez, they established the city of Santa Cruz de la Sierra. Although Chávez was ultimately killed in conflict with the Indians, his name survived in the name of one of the provinces of the modern department of Santa Cruz and among his descendants. One of them, Ñuflo Chavez, was to be a leading political figure and vice-president of Bolivia in the 1950s.

THE ENCOMIENDA AND THE MITA

As they did elsewhere in their conquered American domains, the Spaniards introduced two institutions into Bolivia that were adaptations of those which had developed in Spain during the centuries-long "reconquest" of Spain from the Moors by the Christians. These were the *encomienda* and the *mita*.

The encomienda was a system whereby after a territory had been conquered from the Moors, a Christian nobleman was given control over a certain number of villages with the task of "protecting" the inhabitants and converting them to Christianity. In return, the protected villagers were obliged to pay various kinds of tribute to their protectors. In America, and specifically in Bolivia, the same system was used and adapted. Members of the conquering Spanish armies were granted control over Indian villages whose inhabitants were obliged to work for those possessing the encomienda in return for the blessings of being converted to the Christian religion—blessings which were notable largely for their absence.

A large part of the population of the Altiplano thus came under the control of Spanish conquerers and their descendants. In large areas, the holders of the encomiendas were content to allow the Indians to continue to maintain their communal organizations, so long as they provided the labor and other emoluments that were demanded of them. As the colonial period went on, quite a few Indian communities in Bolivia, as elsewhere in Spanish America, were able to obtain grants from the king, recognizing their right to control their own lands and to manage their own affairs. Many of these communities persisted into the nineteenth century.

With the passage of time, the encomienda, which started out as a temporary grant of land for 20 years, was extended to the lifetime of the holder, and then could be inherited by his heirs. In the early eighteenth century, all surviving encomiendas were converted into outright land grants.

On these holdings there developed the system of exploitation of the land and the Indians that was to survive until the Bolivian National Revolution of

1952. The Indians had small pieces of land for the use of their families in return for work on the rest of the landlord's holdings, combined with an adaptation of the old mita, whereby they had to give additional free labor service to the landowner.

Even the Indians who were able to maintain their traditional ayllu communities were exploited by the provincial authorities, so-called corregidores, appointed by the Audiencia (provincial council), unless the communities were too isolated to be reached even by these authorities. The corregidores were entitled to collect tribute from all male Indians between 18 and 50 years of age, but often collected from all of the Indians, regardless of their age and sex, and kept a large part of what they took for themselves. The corregidores also had a monopoly of goods brought in from the coast for sale to the Indians, and were often in a position to force their "customers" to buy. The Indians were exploited in this way, and Spaniards lucky enough to win favor in the royal court and an appointment in its American empire were able to accumulate substantial fortunes in short periods of time.

Even more damaging to the Indians than the encomienda was the mita. This, too, was an adaptation of an old institution that had grown up in medieval Spain. According to the mita, the members of local Spanish communities had been obliged from time to time to work together on projects of importance to the locality, such as roads, maintenance of irrigation facilities, and the like. For such service the community members did not receive any recompense.

In America, however, the mita soon ceased to be merely a communal enterprise. It was perverted into a system whereby the Indian communities anywhere in the vicinity of the principal silver mining centers were obliged to contribute workers to labor in the mines. Vast numbers of those drafted to work in the mines did not survive. The reaction of many of the Indians was to abandon their traditional homes and move far away from the mining centers. Thus substantial areas near the mining areas were largely depopulated during the colonial period.

The Spanish crown was not unaware of the exploitation of the Indians in Bolivia and elsewhere in the American empire. Starting as early as the 1540s, it began to enact laws designed to protect the Indians from the worst kinds of exploitation. However, these laws were often honored more in the breach than in the execution, and this was particularly the case in Upper Peru, which was a long way indeed from the center of viceregal authority in Lima.

POTOSI

From the Spanish point of view, colonial Bolivia was important for its rich silver mines. The queen of the mines throughout the first century and a half of Spanish rule was the silver mountain of Potosí, which was for a long period the most munificent source of quick wealth—and dire exploitation and poverty—to be found in all of America.

The bittersweet saga of Potosí began in 1545 when an Indian working for a Spaniard named Villarroel accidently discovered a vein of silver near the surface of a very large hill in a desolate part of the Altiplano, at 14,000 feet above sea level. Villarroel soon despoiled his employee of his discovery, and when the nearby Indians sought to assert a claim to a part of what had been found, they were driven off by gunfire of Spaniards. From then on, the Indians labored in the bowels of the mountain mining silver for their Spanish exploiters.

King Charles V was soon informed of the discovery of a fabulous source of silver in the Bolivian Altiplano. He thereupon issued a charter for the Imperial City of Potosí, with a coat of arms picturing the fabulous mountain. Meanwhile, people from all over the empire had descended upon the bleak mining camp which, despite its pomp and circumstance, was the Imperial City of Potosí. It is estimated that more than 40,000 Spaniards, accompanied by 6,000 black and mulatto slaves, and 65,000 Indians, had gathered at the foot of the mountain of silver within a very few years of the discovery of the precious metal. By 1650, the Imperial City had a population of 120,000 and some years subsequently it reached its all-time high of 160,000. At that time, it was the most populous city in all of America.

In 1563 a large mercury deposit was found not far from Potosí. Within a decade, this deposit was being exploited also to provide the ingredient for the mercury amalgamation process that facilitated the extraction of silver from Potosí's mountain. The use of this process intensified the boom of the Imperial City.

The mining camp-city of Potosí remained during its heyday a place of the most glaring contrasts between wealth and dire poverty. The wealth was that of the Spanish owners of the mines, the poverty that of the Indians who were forced to dig into the mountain to despoil it of its hidden treasure.

The mine owners had fortunes that ranged as high as the equivalent of $6 million. They lived amid great pomp and circumstance. Both men and women of the elite wore clothing of silk, replete with gold and precious stones. They entertained themselves with gambling (there were 36 gambling houses in the city at Potosí's prime), bullfighting, balls, banquets, and other fetes. Vast sums were spent on providing the town with a water supply, and the Imperial City prided itself on the expensiveness of the funeral services that were organized at the time of the deaths of King Carlos V and Phillip II.

The Spanish and mestizo elite of the Royal City lived in solidly built stone houses, some 4,000 of which were reported to have existed in 1659. There were also numerous churches, also very well built of stone and richly ornamented by the mine owners.

Violence was characteristic of the Imperial City of Potosí. Not only were there frequent clashes over mining claims occurring in the interior of the mountain, there were almost daily duels in the city itself. Armed bands of soldiers and civilians often made the streets of the city very dangerous. The carrying of weapons in public was virtually universal among the Spaniards, and even among their black and mulatto slaves, while the exalted members of the city council held their meetings clothed in coats of mail, with their swords and pistols at the ready.

The royal treasury also profited handsomely from the mountain of Potosí. Although the crown probably did not receive all of the 20 percent tax on silver that was its due, it did obtain vast quantities of precious metals, with which both Charles V and Phillip II financed their dynastic wars for nearly three-fourths of a century. The silver of Potosí was thus a major factor in freeing the Spanish kings from any dependence on their country's middle class that had led in other European countries to the limitation of the power of the monarchs. It also helped to blind them to the cataclysmic decline of the domestic Spanish economy.

In contrast to the ostentatious wealth of the mine owners and tax collectors was the abysmal poverty of the Indians. They lived in 139 villages in the vicinity of Potosí, and levies of men were required to work several months a year in the mines, while the rest of the year they could devote to their own pursuits. However, a deathrate that often was 80 percent in one year among those working inside the mountain meant the decimation of the Indian communities that were ill-fated enough to live within range of the mine labor recruiters. The only reason the Indian population of the area survived at all was because the royal authorities strictly enforced rules limiting the number of Indians who could be employed in the mines at any one time.

However, the royal city of Potosí declined as dramatically as it had risen. Within a century of the beginning of the silver rush, production had already drastically declined. By the time of the independence of Bolivia, the silver hoard had almost been worked out and the population had dwindled to only about 8,000 souls.

DECLINE OF THE INDIAN POPULATION

Although exact figures are very difficult to come by, there can be no question about the fact that the Indian population in Spanish America declined drastically between the time of the conquest and the middle of the eighteenth century. Certainly, Bolivia was no exception.

Nicolás Sánchez-Albórnoz gives indications that even before the advent of the great mining industry about the middle of the sixteenth century, the Indian population of Spanish America may have declined by as much as 50 percent. It continued to decline for the next two centuries. So drastic did the situation become that the Spanish viceregal authorities in Lima ordered as early as 1575 the consolidation of the Indian population into new communities because of the dwindling numbers of people in the surviving Indian villages.

Sánchez-Albórnoz provides some figures concerning this regroupment of Indians in Upper Peru. These figures show cases in which the number of villages existing on a Spanish-owned landholding was reduced from 33 to two, and even from 134 to 3. Whereas before the regrouping the villages involved had ranged from 44 inhabitants to 548, after the consolidation they varied from an average population of 1,165 to an average of 5,993.

Various explanations have been offered for the decimation of the Indian population in Bolivia and elsewhere in Spanish America during the first two and a half centuries of the colonial period. Probably most important was the spread of diseases with which the Indians had no experience—notably smallpox and measles—brought in by the Europeans as well as by the Africans imported as slaves. Certainly also of importance, particularly in Bolivia, was the excruciatingly hard and debilitating labor conditions in the mines. Finally, Sánchez-Albórnoz insists that the lack of a will to survive on the part of the Indians, reflected in low birthrates relative to the deathrates, was also a major factor in bringing about the decimation of the Indian population.

ANTECEDENTS TO INDEPENDENCE

Throughout the colonial period, Upper Peru was one of the more difficult parts of the Spanish Empire to control effectively. During most of the three centuries of colonial rule, the area was part of the viceroyalty of Peru, with its capital city on the Peruvian coast at Lima. With the reorganization of the Spanish Empire under the Bourbon kings of the eighteenth century, the viceroyalty of the Rio de la Plata, with its seat in Buenos Aires, was established in 1777, and Upper Peru was transferred to its jurisdiction.

Whether under the viceroyalty of Peru or that of the Rio de la Plata, Upper Peru was a long distance from the center of authority. It was very difficult for the Spanish officials to maintain effective control of day-to-day affairs in the area. A lack of "law and order" characterized the Royal City of Potosí during the decades of prosperity.

Most of the Indians who were not directly subjected to the mita of forced service in the mines tended to seek protection by as much isolation as possible from their hated Spanish overlords. But the situation began to change in the last part of the nineteenth century. In Bolivia there were a number of local Indian insurrections that were more or less rapidly suppressed by the Spanish authorities.

Undoubtedly the most serious menace to Spanish authority in that period came from the uprising of Tupac Amaru in 1781. Although the center of this rebellion was the region around Cuzco, some distance from Lake Titicaca, it certainly involved some Indians from Upper Peru, across the lake.

Until his uprising, Tupac Amaru was known as José Gabriel Condorcanqui. He was a well-educated Indian who claimed descent from the sixteenth-century

Indian leader Tupac Amaru, but had indicated himself sufficiently loyal to the Spanish regime to be given the title of Marquis of Oropesa. However, when his efforts to persuade the Spanish authorities to mitigate the harsh treatment he saw being meted out to the Indians came to naught, he raised the banner of rebellion, proclaiming himself Tupac Amaru and announcing the reestablishment of the Inca Empire. Both the viceroy of Peru and the viceroy of Rio de la Plata sent troops to suppress his insurrection, and he was finally captured and brutally executed on May 18, 1781.

However, the penultimate rebellion in Upper Peru against Spanish authority before the general outbreak of the wars of independence was by creoles (American-born descendants of Spaniards) and mestizos of mixed Spanish-Indian ancestry led by Pedro Domingo Murillo. In 1809, they raised the standard of revolt, and proclaimed an independent state in Upper Peru. They were finally overcome by Spanish troops sent from Peru, but some of the rebels continued a guerrilla struggle against the Spanish authorities until the arrival of the liberating armies of Bolívar in 1825.

Murillo is today regarded as the precursor of Bolivian independence. The old Plaza Civica in La Paz, on which are located the presidential palace, the cathedral, and the houses of Congress, was renamed the Plaza Murillo, bearing that name to the present.

4

THE FIRST CENTURY
OF INDEPENDENCE

Bolivia owed its independence as a sovereign state to Simón Bolívar, who not only also provided the country with a name, but also endowed it with its first constitution. However, his efforts to give the country a stable, albeit rather authoritarian, form of government failed catastrophically. As a result, during the first century of its existence as a republic, Bolivia had 40 chief executives, 6 of whom were assassinated while in the presidency, and there were almost 190 armed uprisings, including several more or less sanguinary civil wars. This tradition of alternating chaos and tyranny has been one that has been hard—and so far, impossible—to break during the latter part of the twentieth century.

THE ROLE OF SIMÓN BOLÍVAR

Efforts to involve Upper Peru in the continental struggle for independence were unsuccessful until after the final major incident of that struggle, the Battle of Ayacucho, which took place in neighboring Peru on December 9, 1824, and in which the troops of Simón Bolívar defeated definitively the remnants of the Spanish armies in South America. Several attempted revolts were suppressed by the Spanish authorities. It was only after the Battle of Ayacucho that Bolívar dispatched one of his principal generals, Antonio José de Sucre, to Upper Peru to bring that part of the old viceroyalty under the control of the "patriots." He entered La Paz in February 1825. Independence was officially proclaimed on August 6, 1825.

Soon after Sucre had assumed control of Upper Peru, the Liberator himself arrived there. Bolívar immediately proclaimed the area a separate republic apart from the Peruvian Confederation that he had established in other parts of the old viceroyalty of Peru. A few months later, a more or less elected assembly christened the new state the Republic of Bolivar, and proclaimed the Liberator himself to be its protector and president. Not long afterward, the title was modified to Republic of Bolivia.

Taking advantage of his position as temporary chief executive of the new state, Bolívar endowed it with a new constitution, which he hoped and presumed would provide the country with long-run stability. The constitution provided for a lifetime president, who would not only name his own vice-president, but would also choose his successor. The constitution also proclaimed Roman Catholicism to be the state religion. It provided for a three-house legislative body to be elected by the property owners of the republic, which meant that only about 10 percent of the citizenry had the right to vote. Finally, the Bolivarian constitution of Bolivia provided for a type of local administration based on that established in France during the French Revolution, whereby all local authorities were appointed by the central government.

THE PERIOD OF SANTA CRUZ

Bolívar did not have much time to spend in establishing the new republic that had been named after him. When he left the country late in 1826, General Sucre was elected first president under the constitution that Bolívar had enacted. The armed forces at Sucre's disposal were composed mainly of men from Colombia and Venezuela who were not at all happy about the permanent assignment to the arid Altiplano of Bolivia. When they finally mutinied early in 1829, an army entered the country under the leadership of Peruvian generals Agustín Gamarra and Andrés Santa Cruz, ostensibly to come to Sucre's aid. However, they drove him out of the country, and he went to Ecuador, where he was assassinated soon after by enemies who had followed him from Bolivia. Nevertheless, the memory of Bolivia's first constitutional president is preserved in the name of what had been the city of Chuquisaca, which was rechristened Sucre and remains so to this day.

General Gamarra quickly returned to Peru, where he became president. Power in Bolivia, therefore, remained in the hands of General Santa Cruz. A mestizo, son of a Spanish official, and an Indian relative of Tupac Amaru, Santa Cruz was born in Peru. He had dreams of rebuilding the old Inca Empire, but first he dedicated himself to improving the situation of the country whose president he had become.

During the first ten years of his rule, Santa Cruz took various steps to provide Bolivia with a stable political regime and a prosperous economy. He had the laws of the country codified, paid off the nation's foreign debt, and began a substantial public works program. He also established a number of educational institutions, including a school of medicine and another of fine arts. However, his regime was markedly authoritarian and paternalistic.

In 1836, General Santa Cruz invaded his native country of Peru. He quickly won control of that republic and proclaimed the establishment of the Bolivian-Peruvian Confederation, apparently as a first step toward uniting all of the old Inca Empire. This move was looked upon with dismay by both Argentina, then dominated by Juan Manuel de Rosas, and Chile, led by President Joaquín Prieto and his aggressive cabinet minister Diego Portales. They declared war on the new confederation, and although Santa Cruz was able to defeat the Argentines, he was not as lucky with the Chileans. After three years of war, Santa Cruz was defeated and deposed as president of both Bolivia and Peru. He died in exile.

BOLIVIA IN THE MID-NINETEENTH CENTURY

Bolivia in the middle decades of the nineteenth century was certainly one of the more backward of the new Spanish American republics. Although it still held a long area on the Pacific coast, running from the Chilean frontier, which was only a few score miles from the city of Copiapó, north to the Peruvian frontier a bit beyond the port of Antofagasta, the Altiplano remained the heart of the country. This was true both from a demographic and a political point of view. There the traditional society established during the colonial period remained virtually intact. A small mestizo and near-white elite ruled over the great mass of the Indian peasantry who continued to cultivate the land under semifeudal conditions. Indeed, the situation of the peasantry declined during this period.

Altiplano Bolivia continued to live to a large degree in isolation from the rest of the world. Many days of travel over inadequate roads were necessary to get from La Paz to the Pacific coast provinces. Contact between the Altiplano and the great eastern part of the country, where there were few people and economic activity was minimal, was even more difficult. In the cities of La Paz and Sucre, and a handful of others, there did exist a small middle class and an artisan working class, which produced a large part of the manufactured goods used in the country, protected from foreign competition as they were by transportation difficulties.

Under these circumstances, control of the government was one of the principal sources of quick accumulation of at least moderate wealth. Taxation levied on consumption goods as well as on the still continuing, albeit very modest, silver-mining industry and on the growing guano and nitrate-mining operations along the Pacific coast provided a source of income worth exploitation by ambitious and unscrupulous rulers. And Bolivia had much more than its share of such government leaders between the end of the Bolivian-Peruvian Confederation in 1839 and the outbreak of the War of the Pacific 40 years later.

Soon after the overthrow of President Santa Cruz, the restored Peruvian President Gamarra sought to conquer Bolivia. However, he was defeated by a Bolivian force led by General José Ballivián in 1841. Ballivián drew up a new constitution and ruled for six years. His term in office was an exception for the period, with the president encouraging the country's economic development and enacting legislation that emancipated the few Negro slaves there were in Bolivia.

With the ousting of the government of General Ballivián in 1847, the country began what was perhaps the worst three decades in its history. Two of the most significant chief executives during this period were Manuel Isidoro Belzú and Mariano Melgarejo.

President Belzú, a particularly avaricious and oppressive ruler, remained in power from December 1848 until August 1855. Guillermo Lora has noted that his government was principally significant because it sought and received the support of the artisans of La Paz and other cities, and attempted to bring about reforms on their behalf and that of the Indian peasantry. Even in his farewell speech to Congress, Belzu said of the "lower orders" of artisans and peasants:

> Educate them, instruct them, improve their condition, let them participate in your rights, in keeping with the spirit of the times. Give them security, work and a living wage and then you will have nothing to fear or lament, Americans! Be consistent with the spirit of democracy which you invoked when you declared your independence. [Lora, p. 27]

Some of Belzu's policies to help the artisans and petty merchants were strongly nationalistic. In April 1849, he closed all foreign-owned warehouses in the country, and shortly afterward decreed that all internal trade in the republic should be carried on only by Bolivian nationals. Lora sums up Belzú's objectives by stating that he

> wanted to see all the exploited become property-owners and good citizens who would be a stabilising factor in the life of the nation. But his republic of small property-owners who, through their numbers, would reduce the violence of conflicts between classes, was condemned to failure by the hard facts of the colonial-based economy. One could not hope to build a broad-based democracy on such a fragile basis. [Pp. 28–29]

Probably the worst of all the presidents of this period was Mariano Melgarejo. As commander of the garrison of La Paz, he overthrew his predecessor, José María Acha. When ex-President Belzú returned from exile, successfully aroused his supporters, and seized control of the presidential palace and much of La Paz, Melgarejo went to the Palacio Quemado, pretended to surrender to Belzú, and while embracing him, shot him dead. Then, emerging on the balcony, he announced Belzú's death to the crowd below and asked rhetorically, "And who still lives?"—to which the crowd, which until that moment had been cheering Belzú, replied "Viva Melgarejo!"

Melgarejo was both ruthlessly tyrannical and exceedingly avaricious. He suppressed all municipal councils, dissolved congress, tyrannized over the church, and executed all of his personal enemies that he could. Meanwhile, he lived with exceeding extravagance, spending particularly lavishly on various mistresses to whom he gave public recognition.

To finance all of this, Melgarejo went to extremes. He declared all Indian communities extinct, and sold off many of their lands to the highest bidder. He made a deal with the Chilean government that substantially reduced the Bolivian claims along the Pacific coast, for which he undoubtedly received adequate compensation.

Finally, in 1871, Melgarejo was overthrown in turn. Not long after his ouster, he was murdered, reportedly as a result of a personal feud with the brother of one of his mistresses.

THE STRUGGLE OVER THE PACIFIC COAST

During all of this period, Bolivia was engaged in a losing struggle to maintain control over the segment of the Pacific coast with which she had emerged from the colonial period. This region was sandwiched in between Peru to the north, and Chile to the south, and the principal danger to Bolivian sovereignty came from the south.

There was some argument between Bolivia and Peru over the port of Arica. This was the principal port of entry and exit for goods going to and from Bolivia, and therefore was of great importance. However, it was not within the original area along the ocean that had been claimed by Bolivia. During the war between the two countries after the end of the Bolivian-Peruvian Confederation in 1839, the Bolivian forces under General Ballivian seized control of the port, and at first proclaimed it part of their country. However, this proved untenable, and in 1842 Bolivian troops withdrew forever from Arica.

Much more serious were Bolivia's problems with Chile. Bolivia had emerged to independence claiming a frontier with Chile along the Rio Salado, some distance north of the valley of Copiapó. At the time of independence, actual Chilean settlement, except for a small colony at Paposo (25 degrees south latitude), did not extend north of Copiapó, located at 27 degrees 20 minutes south.

However, several factors favored the extension of Chilean influence north of the original boundary between the two countries. First, Chile, in contrast to Bolivia, was a well-integrated, stably governed country after 1830. Second, it had an aggressive commercial class based on the city of Valparaiso, which was very interested not only in trade but in building up a merchant marine and investing its substantial profits not only within Chile's original borders, but also in regions both to the south and north of those frontiers.

Finally, there existed very substantial economic incentive for the Chileans to extend their influence and then their sovereignty over the coastal portions of Bolivia that were weakly held by the La Paz government. In the earlier decades of the period, the principal economic factor was extensive deposits of guano, that is, bird excrement, on islands along the coast of both Bolivia and Peru. These deposits were very valuable as fertilizer and for other purposes, and European investors as well as Chileans were interested in exploiting them. In addition, in the 1840s very extensive nitrate deposits had been discovered in the Bolivian desert along the Pacific coast. Nitrate, even more than guano, were in great demand in Europe, and the Chilean entrepreneurs, often in partnership with British interests, were very active in opening up the exploitation of these nitrate reserves.

By the middle 1860s, Chile had extended its territorial claims along the coast from the Rio Salado north to 24° south latitude. Bolivia, for its part, had reduced the area over which it claimed sovereignty to the area north of the town of Paposo, on the 24° south latitude line. At this point, Bolivian President Melgarejo struck a "deal" with the Chilean government of President José Joaquín Pérez. According to this arrangement of 1866, it was agreed that the international boundary would be drawn at the twenty-fourth parallel, but that a zone of joint mineral exploitation by both Bolivia and Chile would be established to run from the twenty-third parallel in Bolivian territory to the twenty-fifth parallel in the Chilean part of the region. It was also agreed that the Bolivians would not levy any new taxes on Chilean firms that were exploiting nitrates in Bolivian territory. It was this part of the agreement that was ultimately to provide the Chileans with a casus belli.

The year 1866 was of great importance for two other reasons. First, in that year Chilean entrepreneurs discovered nitrates near the Bolivian port of Antofagasta, thus stimulating Chilean interest in the northern part of the Bolivian littoral. Second, that was the year in which Chile and Bolivia joined Peru and Ecuador in a war against the "mother country" of Spain.

The Spaniards had never recognized the independence of Peru. When, in 1865, the Peruvian government refused to deal with a Spanish "agent" who did not treat their government as a sovereign power in a diplomatic dispute, the Spanish government retaliated by having ships of its fleet seize the Chica Islands, rich in guano, off the Peruvian coast. Peruvian President Mariano Prado thereupon declared war on Spain, and an alliance was hastily formed with Chile, Bolivia, and Ecuador, all of which declared war in January 1866. Valparaiso, Chile, was heavily bombarded by Spanish warships, but the Spanish government found the logistics of such long-range warfare beyond its capacity and withdrew its fleet. A formal truce was signed in 1871 and a treaty was negotiated eight years later.

Meanwhile, relations between Chile and Bolivia had completely broken down. Fearful of Chilean expansionism, Bolivia and Peru had signed a defensive-offensive alliance in 1873. Then, early in 1878, the Bolivian government of Hilarión Daza violated the agreement that Melgarejo had signed by imposing a tax on nitrates exported from the Bolivian part of the joint mineral exportation zone. When one major Chilean company refused to pay this tax, the Daza government ordered the seizure of the company's property and its sale to recoup the amount of the tax as well as ordering the arrest of the company's British manager.

As a consequence of this dispute, Chilean naval forces seized the port of Antofagasta on February 14, 1879, thus commencing the War of the Pacific. Peru immediately entered the conflict on the side of Bolivia, as had been agreed in their treaty of 1873. But the war proved to be a disaster for both of the allies. By the end of 1879, all of Bolivia's coastal area was firmly in Chilean hands. Chilean troops pushed north to occupy the Peruvian port of Arica, and continued further north until they entered the Peruvian capital of Lima in January 1881.

The war finally ended when Peru signed a peace treaty with Chile in 1883 and Bolivia signed a truce with Chile in April 1884. The final adjudication of the Peruvian-Chilean border (as provided in the 1883 treaty) did not take place until 1929, but Bolivia reached agreement with Chile in a treaty signed in 1904. However, the Bolivians never really accepted this treaty, which ceded all of its coastal possessions to Chile; an "outlet to the sea" has remained an issue that succeeding Bolivian dictators have used from time to time to arouse patriotic fervor and hence support for themselves. The most recent to do so was President Hugo Banzer in the 1970s.

THE POSTWAR PERIOD

The catastrophe of the War of the Pacific brought important changes to Bolivia, particularly to its politics. It ended for some time the system of changing governments by a bloody coup d'etat, inaugurated a period of civilian rule, and brought into existence the nation's first political parties.

The Liberal Party was the first to be organized in 1883, drawing its backing principally from the city of La Paz and the mining interests in the northern part of the Altiplano. A year later the Conservative Party, with its major center of strength in Sucre, was organized, representing in large part the mining interests of the southern part of the highlands.

Neither political party was in any sense a mass organization. With one exception, governments changed hands between 1884 and 1920 by election rather than by force. The electorate was extremely limited, only literates being able to vote. Even as late as 1951, only about 3 percent of the population was on the electoral rolls.

The Conservatives were in power from 1884 until 1899. During this period, they carried out modest programs of economic development, encouraging construction of the country's first railroads. They were favorably disposed toward the silver-mining industry, which until the last part of their rule still continued to provide most of the country's exports.

In 1899, the Liberal Party seized power in a short civil war. It was an organization officially committed to nineteenth-century liberalism, encouraging free enterprise, free trade, and foreign investment, particularly in the exploitation of the country's mineral resources.

The victory of the Liberal Party resolved one dispute of long duration: the controversy over whether the capital should officially be moved from Sucre (the old Chuquisaca), which had been the seat of government since the days of the Audiencia de Charcas, to La Paz, near Lake Titicaca and much more accessible to the outside world. The Liberals favored transferring the capital and as a result it was in fact established in La Paz, although until this day Sucre is officially listed as the country's capital. The presidency and the Congress moved to the northern city, and only the Supreme Court—admittedly the least important of the three branches of the Bolivian government—remained in Sucre.

The Liberals were in no sense a government "of the people," as demonstrated by the actions of President Ismael Montes, military leader of the Liberals' seizure of power and president from 1903-09 and 1913-17. Early in the Liberal regime the general, touring the region near Lake Titicaca, came upon one of the surviving Indian communities nearby. Much impressed with the richness of the area that the community occupied, he promptly established his ownership of that land, ordered that all of the members of the Indian community be moved to La Paz, and forbade, under pain of death, any of them to return to their land. Indians from elsewhere were brought in to work the land for General Montes, and it remained a large estate until the agrarian reform of the early 1950s.

THE TIN BOOM

One of the significant aspects of the Liberal victory in 1899 was that it represented a shift of power from the silver-mining interests, still predominant in the Sucre area, to the tin-mining enterprises that were located principally in the northern part of the Altiplano. It signified the definitive victory of the baser metal over the precious.

The name most closely associated with the emergence of tin as the greatest source of wealth and exports in Bolivia is that of Simón Patiño. He began the tin boom and was the one who profited most from it.

Patiño was an Indian, employed as a store clerk at a silver mine near Oruro. On one occasion, he gave a prospector credit, accepting as security the prospector's mining claim. This action and the failure of the prospector to pay his debts brought Patiño's dismissal from the company store, and left him and his wife little to do except to work the claim, which was generally deemed to be worthless.

However, the prospector's claim had no silver on it, but instead had fabulous deposits of tin. At first Patiño and his wife began working the claim almost without any help. However, Patiño was intelligent and wily enough both to know the great value of the property that he had accidentally acquired and to realize that he did not have, and there did not exist in Bolivia, the capital and the technical knowledge necessary to open a major tin-mining operation.

Patiño was able to interest investors in both the United States and Great Britain in his tin-mining enterprise. The firm that he established went through several transformations and finally was organized as the Patiño Mines and Enterprises Consolidated, which was incorporated in the state of Delaware in the United States. From its inception, the Patiño firm was the largest of the enterprises in the tin-mining industry.

Patiño was shrewd enough, in spite of his humble background, not to allow himself to be taken advantage of by the foreign investors whom he interested in his operations. He continued to be a major owner of the firm, and it made him one of the world's wealthiest individuals. From at least the 1920s on, he spent most of his time in Europe. His children, if not Patiño himself, became leading members of European café society. They took even less interest than Patiño had in the welfare of the workers in the mines or in their nation.

However, Patiño was not the only one who capitalized on Bolivian tin. During the last decade of the nineteenth century and the first quarter of the twentieth, a large number of firms entered the tin-mining field. For instance, in 1922 the Guggenheim interests established a firm that quickly became one of the major ones.

For several decades there was a "tin rush" comparable to the gold and silver rushes of the past. The Altiplano was scoured for veins of the now precious mineral. Although the biggest finds were in the Oruro area in the northern part of the Altiplano, deposits were also found in other parts of the highlands. In the Potosí area, old silver mines were searched to find deposits of the new mineral, with only modest results.

By the end of the 1920s, the Bolivian mining industry was largely centered in three firms. The largest of these, of course, was the Patiño enterprise. The other two were the Hochschild firm, dominated by Mauricio Hochschild, an Austrian who had acquired Argentine citizenship, and the Compagnie Aramayo de Mines en Bolivie, controlled by the Aramayo family, who were resident most of the time in Bolivia but were said to be of Colombian origin. Of course, there was British and American capital in the two smaller firms as well as in the Patiño one. It was these three companies that continued to dominate the tin-mining industry and profoundly influence politics until they were finally expropriated after the Bolivian National Revolution in 1952.

The growth of the tin-mining industry was greatly aided by the development of the first railway connections between Bolivia and the outside world in the aftermath of the War of the Pacific. At that time there existed in the coastal area Chile had seized from Bolivia a British-owned railway to serve the nitrate fields near Antofagasta, belonging to the Compania de Salitres y Ferrocarril de Antofagasta. In 1887 the railroad was brought by a British mining firm operating in Uyuni and Oruro, where it worked both silver and tin mines, and in 1888 the Antofagasta (Chili) and Bolivia Railway Company was established, with its corporate center in London. It proceeded in the years that followed to extend the railroad from Antofagasta to Uyuni and Oruro, thus making it possible to ship minerals from the Oruro area directly to the now Chilean port of Antofagasta. The first substantial shipment of tin by rail from the Oruro area was made in 1895. In 1908, the railroad was extended from Oruro to La Paz.

A second major railway connection with the Pacific was built as a result of the Bolivian-Chilean Treaty of Peace, Friendship and Commerce signed in October 1904. According to the terms of the treaty, Chile agreed to construct a railway to La Paz from Arica, the former Peruvian port which the Chileans had occupied but the ultimate sovereignty over which was not decided until 1929. In spite of protests from the Peruvian government over the railway's being built in territory over which it still claimed sovereignty, the Chileans went ahead with the project, the Bolivian section of which was finally completed in 1913 but was not turned over to the Bolivian government until 1928. J. Valerie Fifer has summed up the story of that road: "Thus a Chilean railway, built for Bolivia, in Peruvian territory, by a British company, put Arica within twenty-four hours of the edge of La Paz" (P. 67).

Some other parts of the country were also connected by railway. In 1911, a spur of the Antofagasta railroad was completed to Potosí, and in 1913 another was finished to Atocha. In 1917, a spur was completed between Oruro and Cochabamba.

Developments outside of Bolivia also served as a major spur to the growth of the Bolivian tin-mining industry for a generation or more. The discovery of the vacuum-packed can as a means for preserving many kinds of food created a very large demand for the tin that was a principal ingredient of such a can. The rise of the automobile industry, which used a substantial amount of tin for various components, provided further demand. In addition, there was a growing variety of other industrial uses for the metal that, until the last years of the nineteenth century, had seemed to be of no practical value at all.

THE ROSCA

By introducing technological innovations into Bolivia and stimulating the growth of such cities as Oruro and La Paz, the tin boom for several decades seemed to solidify rather than to weaken the old order in the country. Bolivia continued to be dominated by what was popularly known as the "Rosca." The precise meaning of the word is not always clear. However, as used by scholars and politicians it generally means the economic and social powers-that-be which for long dominated the economy, social life, and politics of Bolivia.

Two of these elements were of particular importance: the landed oligarchy, with its roots in the colonial era, and the new tin-mining interests. Although these two groups had certain divergent interests, they were firmly united in trying to prevent any major changes in the status quo.

The cultivated land, particularly in the Altiplano and the Yungas, continued to be in the hands of the large landholders. Most of them continued to have their holdings cultivated by Indian peasants who worked on shares or under arrangements not unlike those of the manorial system of medieval Europe. Their principal concern was that nothing should be done to imperil their control of the land and the people who worked on it.

The tin-mining firms, although allied politically and otherwise with the landed oligarchy, were markedly different from them in many ways. First, they represented the modern world economy, in contrast to the landowners, whose system was an adaptation of the feudal economy and society. Second, most of the "tin barons" were upstarts, johnny-come-latelies, symbolized by Simon Patiño, the humble Indian who had struck it rich. Finally, the tin-mining interests included among their number substantial elements from outside of Bolivia. Not only were the big mining companies partly owned by foreigners from Europe and the United States, but these companies employed substantial numbers of foreign technicians, engineers, and managers.

The people dominating the tin-mining firms were as interested as the landowners in seeing that there were no fundamental changes in the status quo. However, their specific concerns were somewhat different from those of the landlords. They wanted to make sure naturally that no attempt was made to deprive them of their rich properties. But at least until after the Chaco War of the 1930s that seemed quite a remote possibility. Immediately the tin barons were concerned with such issues as being able to do as they wished with the foreign exchange that their firms earned by selling their product abroad, maintaining a profitable price for their product, and perhaps most urgently, maintaining the draconian control that they exercised over the people who worked in the mines.

Conditions in the mines were reprehensible at best. The mining camps were isolated, and were under the complete control of the mining companies. The workers lived in company houses, and bought in company stores ("pulperias"); the companies supplied whatever educational or medical facilities were available. The wages the workers received were often paid in chits on the company stores rather than in cash, and debts to the pulperías tied the workers indissolubly to their jobs. The companies had their own police, and had the custom of supplementing the pay of the low-ranking government officials who were stationed in or near the mining camps to assure their "cooperation" in any emergency that might arise with the workers.

Aside from the problems of isolation and iron control by the employers, the workers faced other deplorable conditions. The housing generally was inadequate if not downright bad. The conditions in the mines were perilous for the workers, not only because of frequent accidents but because the dust and other impurities in the air in the mines almost guaranteed that after a given number of years the workers would be victims of silicosis and similar diseases. Finally, the wages received by the workers—recruited originally from the Indian peasant population—were meager in the extreme, rarely enough to cover their debts to the pulperías.

The tin barons whose operations were, until the mid-1920s at least, highly profitable were understandably unwilling to see the government interfere in any way with the manner in which they ran their businesses. They joined with the rural landowners to work behind the scenes, and sometimes more openly, to assure that there were in-power governments, of whatever party affiliation, that would not take any moves to challenge the mine owners' sovereignty in the mining camps and their ability to dispose of their foreign exchange as they wished, but would also provide them the services that they might need from the State. Until the Chaco War, the Rosca succeeded in diverting any efforts to upset the status quo, and even for 17 years after the end of that conflict succeeded in preventing any major changes. More than one president found out too late how perilous it was to challenge the Rosca.

The Rosca not only dominated the nation's economy and politics, but also constituted the social elite. The top officials of the mining enterprises mixed with the large landholders, some of the wealthier merchants, and a sprinkling of the top leaders of the government service and officer corps of the military to form the "society" of Bolivia. They had exclusive clubs in La Paz and other cities, lavishly entertained one another, and financed splendid weddings for their daughters.

The wealthier members of the Rosca, particularly from the mining and commercial interests, spent longer or shorter periods abroad, mixing with the social elites of Europe and the United States. Some, like the Patiños, seldom saw their native country except to visit there occasionally.

Life was indeed good for the Rosca. They monopolized power, possessed great wealth, and constituted a major part of the educated population at the expense of the great mass of the people—the Indian peasants, the Indian and semi-Indian miners, and the humbler elements of the cholo population of the major cities. Only with the fissures opened up in national life by the catastrophe of the Chaco War was this system of domination by the Rosca to begin to crumble. The beginnings of revolt against the system started in the few decades preceding the war.

THE ROLE OF THE MILITARY

Until the Chaco War, a key to the Rosca's control of Bolivia was its influence with the military. Although the military on various occasions overthrew the government in power, it generally allowed the civilians to run the government, and was virtually immune to any ideas of changing fundamentally the country's economic, social, and political institutions. Although notoriously incapable of protecting the nation's frontiers when they were endangered, the military was very effective in preventing the upsurge of any serious challenge to the status quo. Only with the shattering experience of the defeat in the Chaco War did the attitude of at least the younger officers begin to change.

Until the second decade of this century, the Bolivian military was quite modest. In 1905 there were only 2,890 members of the armed forces. The 1910 edition of the *Encyclopedia Britannica* notes:

> The enrolled force is, however, both unorganized and unarmed. The strength of the army is fixed in each year's budget. That for 1903 consisted of 2933 officers and men, of which 275 were commissioned and 558 non-commissioned officers, 181 musicians, and only 1906 rank and file. A conscription law of 1894 provides for a compulsory military service between the ages of twenty-one and fifty years, with two years actual service in the regulars for those between twenty-one and twenty-five, but the law is practically a dead letter.

One factor that helped to assure the armed forces would remain stalwart supporters of conditions as they were was the fact that during most of the 20 years before the outbreak of the Chaco War they were under foreign leadership. This had begun in January 1911 when a German military mission under the leadership of Major Hans Kundt, detailed for the purpose by the German General Staff, arrived in Bolivia to train the Bolivian armed forces. Kundt virtually took command of the Bolivian army. Although he went back to Germany during World War I, he returned to Bolivia in 1919. Although not having the title, Kundt was virtually the commander of the Bolivian armed forces and he had various other German officers under him, including for a time Captain Ernst Roehm, who later was the organizer and head of the notorious Nazi SA paramilitary gangs.

Fifer has noted that "Kundt was generally regarded as the strong man behind the Saavedra Administration (1920-1925), although as a professional soldier, bent almost exclusively upon creating a new, well-disciplined army from a small officer-elite and a groundmass of Indian laborers, his purpose, he declared, was to keep out of politics" (pp. 205-6). He also notes that "by 1924 the army comprised about ten thousand men. . . ."

German military men continued to be in control of the armed forces until after the outbreak of the Chaco War. With the first major defeats in that conflict, however, they were quickly eliminated, to be substituted by Bolivian officers who equaled them in incompetence and surpassed them in corruption.

THE REPUBLICAN PARTY

One of the first evidences of discontent with the existing state of affairs was the rise of the Republican Party. This party was a peculiar amalgam of lower and lower middle class people of the cities, with segments of both the agricultural and mining sectors of the Rosca.

Until the victory of the Liberal Party in the civil war of 1899, the artisans and small businessmen of La Paz and other cities had tended to support the Liberal Party. However, during its years in power, the Liberal Party became increasingly associated with the magnates of the tin-mining industry, and less and less concerned with the interests of its artisan and petty-bourgeois partisans.

The founding of the Republican Party in 1914, under the leadership of Bautista Saavedra, reflected the disillusionment of the lower class Liberals. They generally turned to the new party, which promised a variety of reforms on their behalf. The Republican Party also found recruits from among the ranks of the old Conservative Party, which after its defeat in 1899 had virtually ceased to exist. Undoubtedly, a principal motivation in their attachment to the Republicans was their hope that this new group would be a vehicle for ousting the hated Liberals from power. Even Patiño, for personal reasons connected with the politics within the mining sector of the Rosca, also gave some support to the Republicans, at least in the beginning.

World War I had a considerable impact on the Bolivian economy. It stimulated the demand for the country's principal export, tin, but also tended to make it difficult to import the consumer goods that the country by then had become accustomed to bringing in from outside. Although serving as an impetus to the establishment and expansion of manufacturing, both by artisans and in factories, this latter effect also stimulated inflation and increased discontent among artisans and working-class people in the cities. These factors added fuel to the Republican fire.

Finally, in July 1920, the Republicans seized power in a virtually bloodless coup d'etat. Saavedra became president. Guillermo Lora, the Trotskyite leader and historian of the Bolivian labor movement, has stated about the regime that

> Saavedra deserves some credit for his efforts to draw up a coherent body of social legislation in an attempt to catch up with the achievement of economically more advanced societies, and for his willingness to make the government more responsible to the growing demands of the underprivileged sectors of society. His government

introduced compensation for industrial accidents, a compulsory savings-scheme and an improved strike law, and set up the Institute of Social Reform. . . . [P. 110]

However, the Saavedra government did little to encourage the organization of the workers, particularly the miners. On various occasions troops were used against strikes. In June 1923 when the miners of Uncia went on strike and organized a large demonstration in front of the subprefect's office after their principal leaders were arrested, troops opened fire upon the workers, killing a large number and wounding many others. This event has gone down in Bolivian labor history as "the massacre of Uncia," and remained a blot on the record of President Saavedra.

The Saavedra government came into office shortly before the post-World War I depression. This economic crisis brought about a drastic decline in tin prices, and brought the government to the verge of bankruptcy. In a desperate attempt to remedy the situation, the Saavedra government contracted loans from U.S. banks that were in terms drastically unfavorable to Bolivia, but Saavedra felt he had little alternative. These loans were used to finance the ordinary expenses of the government until tin prices at least partially recovered and some of the money was expended on various public works projects.

In 1925, Saavedra was succeeded as president by Hernando Siles, a bitter political opponent of Saavedra although also a Republican. He finally organized his own Nationalist Party, recruiting a number of young nationalist-minded intellectuals, a few of whom many years later were to play a role in the MNR. Siles was also able to rally considerable support among the workers, including some of the miners.

The Siles government continued the policies of its predecessor insofar as floating very large loans abroad was concerned. This made the government's situation all the more desperate when, at the end of 1929, the Great Depression broke very quickly having a disastrous impact on the mining industry and other monetized parts of the Bolivian economy. Siles was no more able than the rulers of most other countries to deal with this economic catastrophe, and in June 1930 he became its victim when his government was overthrown and succeeded by a military junta.

New elections were soon held, and a third president from the Republican Party ranks was chosen. This was Daniel Salamanca, who had been the most persistent rival of Saavedra within the Republican ranks and had organized his own Genuine Republican Party against the faction headed by Saavedra, which took the name Socialist Republican Party. It was the Salamanca government that led the country into the Chaco War, bringing about the end (with the exception of the 1946–51 period) of the rule of the Republican Party and preparing the way for very fundamental changes in the economy and society—and for a while in the politics—of Bolivia.

THE BEGINNINGS OF THE REVOLT AGAINST THE STATUS QUO

The artisans of La Paz and some other cities had for long maintained mutual benefit societies that were political vehicles for their class and sometimes engaged in electoral activity on their own or in support of one or another national party faction. The Federación Obrera of La Paz had been closely aligned with the Liberal Party. With the onset of disillusionment in the Liberals among the artisans, its rival, the Federación Obrera Internacional, was sympathetic to the Republican Party.

After World War I, the activities of the organized workers intensified, and they began to extend to important new groups, particularly the railroad workers and the miners. In August 1919, the first union of railroad workers was established, the Liga de Obreros y Empleados de Ferrocarril, including workers on the railroad to Antofagasta and that from La Paz to Lake Titicaca. In the following year, the former group established its own Federación Ferroviaria, which until the Chaco War remained one of the country's major workers' organizations. The Federación organized a general strike in January 1921 that was finally settled after President Saavedra negotiated with the workers and agreed to enact several important pieces of labor leigislation.

The miners in various parts of the country—Uncia, Oruro, and elsewhere— also began to establish unions. However, the attitude of successive governments toward these organizations was much more severe than toward the railroad and city workers' groups. During the period before the Chaco War, the miners were unable to establish any effective national federation.

New political tendencies began to develop among the organized workers in the 1920s. During most of the period, Marxists of various views tended to dominate many of the labor groups, particularly the federations that were established in a number of cities. Small Communist groups appeared in several cities, and in 1928 a clandestine Communist Party, which professed to be national in scope but in fact had only a handful of members, was established on the direct orders of the Communist International.

The most famous Bolivian Marxist-Leninist in the 1920s was undoubtedly Gustavo Navarro, who was more generally known by his pseudonym Tristán Marof. He had begun his political career as a Republican, participating in the 1920 Republican revolution. Subsequently, he had been named by President Saavedra as Bolivian consul in Genoa. During this diplomatic stint, he converted to Marxism-Leninism and wrote the book *La Justicia del Inca*, which although published in Belgium circulated widely in Bolivia. Of this volume Lora comments, "In his book . . . the slogan 'Land to the people, mines to the state,' appeared for the first time. For decades these words exuded a certain magic and were used as a rallying cry. The workers congress of 1927 adopted them as their slogan" (p. 165).

When Marof returned home to Bolivia in 1927, he went on a lecture tour around the country preaching Marxist-Leninist ideas. Finally arrested, he was deported to Mexico and remained in exile until after the end of the Chaco War.

Near the end of the 1920s, the anarchists gained substantial influence in the labor movement. They established the Federación Obrera Local, which included not only artisans and some other workers in the city of La Paz but some peasants from nearby Altiplano areas. During the years immediately preceding the Chaco War, this was perhaps the strongest single labor group in the country. It resurfaced after that conflict, but never again had the influence it enjoyed in the late 1920s.

The beginnings of an organized labor movement were not the only indications of discontent with the rule of the Rosca. A student movement also appeared during the 1920s. The first student federation was established at the University of Cochabamba in 1925 and in August 1928 the first national student congress was held in Cochabamba to establish the national Federación Universitaria Boliviana (FUB). Lora has noted that

> There were three main influences on the FUB: the university reform movement which started in Cordoba, Argentina, and spread throughout the continent; the Russian revolution, whose influence reached Bolivia through the propaganda and activities of the communist parties in Latin America; and finally, the Bolivian labor movement which was then setting up trade unions and proposing a class-based party. [P. 147]

Several people who played important parts in establishing the student movement were to become important political leaders in the post–Chaco War period. These included José Antonio Arce, Ricardo Anaya, and José Aguirre Gainsborg, among others. Most of the student leaders were, as Lora comments, "moving towards Marxism."

Finally, there were evidences of considerable restlessness among the Indian peasantry. In August 1927 there was a large-scale Indian uprising. Lora describes the uprising:

> . . . about a hundred thousand peasants in Cochabamba, Potosí and Sucre rose up in revolt against the authorities and the landowners. In the department of Cochabamba thirty thousand peasants gathered together around Vacas Tiraque. The authorities and landowners fled the district, and the landowners demanded the government's protection. Around Sucre the peasants were crushed when the army general staff turned their machine guns on the protestors. In the Altiplano the repression was even more brutal. Eight thousand soldiers of the Camacho regiment set out from Oruro to "restore order" to the large haciendas and the peasant communities. The foreign press agency, UP, reported that "there was only one death among the

soldiers and the whites, but more than 200 Indians were killed."
[Pp. 144–45]

After 1929 the mass organizations suffered severe blows. The Great Depression created economic conditions that undermined the bargaining power of labor unions, and the government of President Salamanca that came to power in 1930 was much less inclined to court them than his two predecessors had been.

But it was the Chaco War that temporarily destroyed the organized labor movement in Bolivia. The government of Salamanca, once the war had begun, ruthlessly suppressed the labor movements of both Communist and anarchist orientation, and likewise largely destroyed the student organizations. Large numbers of labor and student leaders were jailed, and many more fled into exile. From 1932 until the fall of Salamanca in 1934, the labor movement virtually ceased to exist. It was to revive under very different circumstances once the Chaco War had ended.

BOLIVIAN FOREIGN RELATIONS

Throughout the first three decades of the century, Bolivia had continuing difficulties with its neighbors. Ultimately, the problems with one of the states on its frontier, Paraguay, led to the Chaco War, opening a whole new phase in the country's history.

In 1903 Bolivia suffered its largest single loss of claimed national territory. This was in the northeastern area known as Acre, and was the result of the rubber boom that had developed in the region in the years previous. Bolivian control over the area was tenuous at best, and with the rubber boom tens of thousands of people moved into Acre from Brazil in search of rubber. They chafed at Bolivian attempts to collect taxes and to exercise authority over them. The Brazilian settlers finally used the excuse of a contract that the Bolivian government had made with an American speculative firm to "develop" the rubber industry of the Acre area as an excuse for revolting. The rebels established what they called the Republic of Acre and promptly applied to Brazil for admission as a state. Although Brazil was not willing to give them the status of a new state, it was quite willing to take over the territory in dispute and promptly did so. In March 1903, Bolivia recognized this acquisition of its territory by its neighbor in the Treaty of Petropolis, signed in the Brazilian summer capital.

In the following year, Bolivia suffered another humiliation when it finally formally recognized the cession of the territory that Chile had taken from it in the War of the Pacific, almost a generation before. In return for finally granting title to what Chile controlled in any case, Bolivia received a financial payment and the promise to build a railroad from Arica to La Paz.

Five years after the definitive settlement of the War of the Pacific, Bolivia settled a pending frontier problem with Peru. The easternmost border between the two countries had never been demarcated. An arbitration award by the Argentine government in 1909 was rejected by the Bolivian government, and after some further negotiations with the Peruvians an agreement was finally reached. According to it, Bolivia ceded considerable territory over which it had claimed but not exercised sovereignty, but this cession was considerably less than that which the Argentine award had originally suggested.

There remained the frontier argument with Paraguay. This festered throughout the first three decades of the twentieth century, and in 1932 resulted in open warfare. After the Chaco War Bolivia was never to be the same.

5

THE CHACO WAR
AND ITS AFTERMATH

Militarily, the Chaco War was an unmitigated disaster for Bolivia. However, in the long run, its impact was positive in a social and political sense. It set afoot a process that was to culminate in the National Revolution of 1952 and to change fundamentally the country's institutions.

CAUSES AND PROGRESS OF THE CHACO WAR

The casus belli of the conflict between Bolivia and Paraguay in the 1930s was a problem similar to that faced by many of the other Spanish-American countries. It was the fact that during the three centuries of Spanish domination of much of America, the boundaries between the various parts of the Spanish Empire had frequently remained vague and undefined. So long as all of the region was under the control of the Spanish crown, there was no urgency about defining such frontiers.

However, once the Spanish-American countries achieved their independence from Spain, the question of boundaries acquired considerable importance. Bolivia had been faced with this issue not only concerning its border with Paraguay, but with those facing Chile, Argentina, and Peru as well. During the nineteenth century, the issues with all of the neighbors except Paraguay had been more or less definitively settled—almost always to Bolivia's disadvantage. However, the border dispute with Paraguay persisted.

The area at issue certainly did not seem an inviting one. It was the region known as the Gran Chaco, parts of which were shared (and are still shared) by

Bolivia, Paraguay, and Argentina. It is a tropical region, dry, barren, and quite inhospitable to man. However, it was known that in the neighboring Santa Cruz region of Bolivia there were petroleum reserves that were already being exploited, and it was widely supposed that there were vast oil resources also in the Chaco area in dispute. One favorite argument at the time of the Chaco War and since has been that rival international oil interests egged the two combatants on, with the British favoring and supporting Paraguay, and the U.S. companies backing Bolivia.

It may well be true that the international oil companies saw possibilities of benefiting from the victory of one or the other of the contestants in the Chaco War. However, the conflict almost certainly would have occurred in spite of any oil firm's interest in it. Ever since the independence of the two countries there had been disputes over the Chaco region, and sometimes these had resulted in local military clashes. The most recent of these before the actual outbreak of the Chaco War had taken place in 1928, when full-scale conflict was only barely avoided.

Once all-out war between Bolivia and Paraguay loomed, it was almost universally supposed that Bolivia would be the easy winner in such a conflict. It was thought to have one of the largest armies in South America, trained for many years by a German military mission, and it was commanded at the time hostilities commenced by a German general. Bolivia was larger in population and was thought to be richer in resources than its opponent. Furthermore, only two generations before Paraguay had fought the devastating War of the Triple Alliance with Brazil, Argentina, and Uruguay that had resulted in the death of almost all Paraguayan males over 14 years of age and from which the country had not yet fully recovered.

However, it was Paraguay that won the war, not Bolivia. There were many reasons for this. Undoubtedly incompetence and corruption in the high command of the Bolivian armed forces had much to do with the outcome of the war. But so did the fact that the conflict was being fought principally by Indian soldiers, conscripted in the cold, oxygen-scarce Altiplano to fight in the hot tropical, almost sea level plains of the Chaco where everything was foreign to them. Far removed from their bases of supply, they lacked almost everything, from adequate armaments to sufficient food. Most of all, they lacked adequate water supplies, their commanders not having taken sufficiently into account the parched nature of much of the terrain over which the soldiers were to fight. To the Indian recruits, there was only an excessively abundant supply of heat, snakes, insects, and other varmints with which they had until then no acquaintance. Bolivian casualties due to disease, snakebite, and thirst far exceeded those due to battle wounds.

While the Bolivian troops suffered defeat after defeat at the hands of their enemies, major international efforts were mounted to try to bring peace between the two countries. The League of Nations, the Pan American Union, and many individual countries became involved in these negotiations. Finally, exhaustion of the two sides, more than brilliant diplomacy on the part of the foreign mediators, brought an end to the conflict late in 1935, when an agreement for a truce, to be followed by a peace treaty, was finally signed in Buenos Aires.

IMMEDIATE IMPACT OF THE CHACO WAR

The Chaco War had a profound effect on Bolivia. Most immediately influenced were those who were taking part in the actual conflict. Both officers and enlisted men felt the impact of the national disaster.

The lower ranking officers were drawn largely from the middle and upper middle classes. These young men suffered alongside their troops the privations of the campaigns, and they were better able to understand than were the common soldiers the incompetence and avarice that were part of the explanation for the failure of Bolivian arms. Many of them came to blame the disaster not only on the Army leadership that was immediately responsible for carrying on the war, but also on the civilian rulers who had led Bolivia into the conflict in the first place. They began to question the whole social, economic, and political system which they conceived had made possible such a bloody defeat.

As for the rank-and-file soldiers, the Indians, they too were deeply influenced by what happened in the Chaco, but their reactions, in political terms, were slower in coming than were those of the young officer group. For many of the young Indian recruits, the war had introduced them to a whole new world—or series of worlds—of which they had not even dreamed before. On the way to the front they passed through cities where life was completely different from what they were accustomed to. For the first time in their lives, they were wrenched from the isolation that the Bolivian Indians had purposefully maintained as a protection against the incursions of the white man of the cities. Such experiences could not help but have a profound impact on the thinking of the Indian recruits, and ultimately on their actions.

Immediately, the only obvious effect of the war on the average Indian was an apparently superficial one. Whereas until then the Bolivian Indians, like their Peruvian cousins, had tended to wear traditional Indian clothing, this changed for the males after the Chaco War. Upon being demobilized, each soldier was given one suit of "store-bought" clothing of the European style—pants, shirt, coat, and so forth—and henceforward the Bolivian Indian male continued to wear that kind of raiment instead of the traditional Indian clothing.

The discontent of the soldiers on all levels with the conduct of the war and the government first found political expression in November 1934 when President David Salamanca was deposed by the military, led by Colonel David Toro, and Vice-President José Luis Tejada Sorzano replaced him. Although the new president finally authorized the signing of an agreement ending the war in

June 1935, the soldiers were not satisfied with his conservative orientation. As a result, on May 13, 1936, President Tejada Sorzano was deposed in turn. Power was taken by a Civilian-Military Junta, which proclaimed Colonel Toro the new president of Bolivia, thus beginning a long period of military control of the government.

The Toro regime proclaimed itself a "Socialist" government. It established for the first time a Ministry of Labor, and filled the post with an old trade unionist, Waldo Alvarez. Subsequently, it expropriated the petroleum concessions of the Standard Oil Company of New Jersey, in part in retribution for the supposed encouragement that Standard Oil had given to the Chaco War. The regime also established the State Socialist Party to be the political expression of the revolution that was supposedly underway.

However, discontent continued among the soldiers on active service and the recently demobilized young officers. As a consequence, in July 1937 there was a further coup d'etat that placed Colonel Germán Busch in the presidency. Busch, one of the few real heroes of the Chaco War, has gone down in Bolivian history as one of the symbols of the Bolivian National Revolution, although his efforts toward change in the late 1930s proved to be abortive.

The Busch government called elections for a new constitutional assembly, and among those elected to this body were several who would play major parts in the country's history in the decades to follow. These included Víctor Paz Estenssoro, Augusto Cespedes, and Walter Guevara Arze, all of whom were to figure among the founders of the Movimiento Nacionalista Revolucionario.

The constitutional assembly, after modifying the country's basic document, elected Busch as constitutional president for a period of four years. However, in April 1939, he dissolved congress and proclaimed himself a dictator.

Meanwhile, the Busch regime had been moving to carry out much more profound reforms than its predecessor. It issued the country's first labor code, which came to be known as the Codigo Busch. However, even more significantly, it began to move against the powerful economic interests that had so long dominated the country.

The Busch government nationalized both the Central Bank and the Mining Bank (Banco Minero), which was a major factor in financing the mining industry. Paz Estenssoro was named as head of the Banco Minero, and Walter Guevara Arze was made one of the members of its Executive Council.

Most significant of all, on June 7, 1939, President Busch issued a decree that reportedly had been drafted by Paz Estenssoro according to which all of the mining companies had to sell to the Central Bank all foreign exchange earned by selling their products abroad. They were also required to give the government detailed accounts of any expenditures of foreign exchange that they made abroad in the conduct of their business.

This decree hit at the heart of the Rosca, particularly the mining oligarchy that since the early years of the twentieth century had been the most powerful political force in the country. The decree met with wide popular support, with large demonstrations organized in the Plaza Murillo in front of the presidential palace to show this backing. However, as might have been expected, it met with violent opposition from the mining companies, particularly the "big three"— Patiño, Aramayo, and Hochschild.

On August 23, 1939, President Busch died of a gunshot wound. The official story at the time was that he had committed suicide. However, there were many then and later who felt that he had probably been murdered in retaliation for his decrees against the mining magnates. Paz Estenssoro once claimed that until he himself became president, he had always supposed that Busch had been murdered, but only upon becoming president had he come to realize that it was possible that a chief executive might want to end his own life.

FORMATION OF NEW POLITICAL PARTIES

Upon the death of President Busch, General Carlos Quintanilla was placed in the presidency by the military leadership. One of his first acts was to cancel the decree concerning the sale of foreign exchange by the mining companies. Quintanilla continued in the presidency until the election of General Enrique Peñaranda, supported by backers of the status quo later in the year.

However, the continued pressure for fundamental changes in the country's economy, society, and polity was reflected in the formation of several new political parties, all of which, in one way or another, challenged the status quo. The most important of these parties were the Falange Socialista Boliviana, the Partido de Izquierda Revolucionaria (PIR), the Partido Obrero Revolucionario (POR), and most important of all, the MNR.

The Falange Socialista Boliviana was established in 1937 by a group of Bolivian exiles then residing in Chile. It was a frankly Fascist-oriented party, patterned more or less on the Spanish Falange of José Antonio Primo de Rivera. It consisted principally of intellectuals and had some contacts among the military officers. However, it remained a small party until after the revolution of 1952, when it became the principal focus of right-wing opposition to the revolutionary regime.

The core of the group that was to form the POR was also established by a number of Bolivian exiles. Known as the Tupac Amaru Group, these young men gathered in Argentina during the Chaco War under the leadership of Gustavo Navarro (Tristán Marof). Navarro was by then an adherent of Leon Trotsky, and the Tupac Amaru Group, therefore, had Trotskyist inclinations from the beginning.

The POR was established in 1934 by members of the Tupac Amaru Group, with Tristán Marof as its leader. However, after Navarro's return to Bolivia, the POR leadership accused him of opportunism. From its inception, the POR was a part of Trotsky's Fourth International. Its leader after Navarro was José Aguirre Gainsborg, who had been one of the exiles in Argentina. However, he was killed in an accident in October 1938. By the end of the decade of the 1940s, Guillermo Lora, a rather fanatical young intellectual with some following in the mining camps, had emerged as the principal figure in the POR.

When Tristán Marof returned to Bolivia early in the Busch administration, he established there the Partido Socialista Obrero Boliviano (PSOB). During the Busch period and for some time thereafter, it undertook to try to establish a trade union organization among the tin miners, and took a leading role in establishing the Miners Federation. In the early 1940s, however, the PSOB lost influence among the miners to the MNR and the POR.

Whereas the POR was Trotskyist, the PIR represented the Stalinist Communist trend. It was established in 1940 as the result of a conference of representatives of a number of small left-wing groups made up principally of intellectuals. Although it proclaimed itself to be "independent Marxist," its inclinations were Stalinist, and it soon established contacts with orthodox Communist parties in a number of other countries, including the United States. Its principal leader in the 1940s was José Antonio Arce, perhaps the country's most outstanding sociologist and a professor in the University of San Andrés in La Paz, who gained the party immediate attention by being the only candidate to run against General Enrique Peñaranda in the presidential election of 1940. Other important figures in the PIR included Ricardo Anaya of the University of Cochabamba, Fernando Sinani, and one of the country's leading literary figures, the novelist Jesús Lara.

The PIR had influence in the fledgling labor movement that had begun to expand after the end of the Chaco War and the advent of professedly reformist governments thereafter. Most of the leaders of the new national labor confederation, the Confederación Sindical de Trabajadores Bolivianos, were members of the PIR by 1943, and the party was particularly strong among the railroad workers.

The most important party to appear during the post–Chaco War period was the MNR. At its inception, it was a rather heterogeneous party, ideologically speaking. It was pronouncedly nationalist, and some of its older leaders had participated in the Nationalist Party of President Hernando Siles in the 1920s. There were undoubtedly some of the founding fathers of the MNR who had sympathy for the Axis powers, particularly for their opposition to the British and the Americans. However, there were others, like Walter Guevara Arze, who were proclaimed Marxists, although not loyal to any particular strain of Marxism.

As we have seen, some of the founders of the MNR had participated in the administration of President Busch. However, it was not until 1941 that they organized as a separate political party. Among the founders of the party were Víctor Paz Estenssoro, Hernán Siles (a son of the former president), Walter Guevara Arze, and Luis Peñaloza, a one-time member of the Tupac Amaru

Group. In 1940 several of these people had been elected to Congress, and after its formal establishment, the MNR became the major critic of the Peñaranda government in parliament.

THE CATAVI MASSACRE

All of these new parties seemed somewhat out of the mainstream of national politics until December 1943. The government and Congress were controlled by the traditional Liberals and the various factions into which the Republican Party had fragmented. General Peñaranda was an essentially conservative president who in no way sought to emulate his predecessors, Colonels Toro and Busch.

Of course, World War II had commenced in September 1939, and the strategic importance of Bolivia as one of the principal producers of tin grew as the war progressed. This was particularly the case after the extension of the war to the Far East following Pearl Harbor and the capture by the Japanese of tin-producing areas in Malaya and elsewhere.

The United States was very anxious to have the greatest possible access to Bolivian tin. General Peñaranda's government was perfectly willing to oblige. However, the very interest of the U.S. economic warfare experts in the Bolivian tin industry tended to center attention on the labor conditions in the mines. This preoccupation was intensified as a result of what came to be known as the Catavi Massacre.

This event occurred in December 1942 as the result of strikes and demonstrations at the Catavi mine, not far from the city of Oruro. In one demonstration, in which numerous women and children participated, troops opened fire on the demonstrators, killing a substantial number and wounding others. This case immediately became a cause célèbre, both in Bolivia and internationally.

The Catavi Massacre provided a major opportunity for the MNR to establish strong contacts with the miners, its first major entry into the labor movement. Delegates from the miners' union came to La Paz looking for support for their cause and a chance to confront the government's policies toward the mine workers. They contacted the MNR members of Congress, and those parliamentarians not only interrogated the government ministers about the Catavi incident, but also gave the party a chance to criticize extensively the general economic and social policies of the Peñaranda government.

Meanwhile, the Catavi Massacre also provoked a strong international reaction. As a result, the United States government dispatched a mission that included organized labor representatives to Bolivia to look into labor conditions in the tin mines. It rendered a very critical report, and suggested that if production of tin was to be maximized for the war effort this would require marked improvements in conditions of the workers in the mining camps.

THE DECEMBER 1943 COUP

In retrospect, it is clear that the Catavi Massacre greatly weakened the position of the conservative Peñaranda government. However, another year passed before it was overthrown.

The insurrection that ousted the Peñaranda regime was a joint effort of a group of young military men and the MNR. The military faction consisted of members of the Marshal Santa Cruz Lodge, known also as the Radepa, which included a substantial number of young nationalistic officers, the principal leader of whom was Major Gualberto Villarroel. It had been organized in the wake of the Chaco War and reflected the discontent of many of the officers with the economic and social status quo and the traditional role of the military as defenders of the Rosca.

The coup occurred on December 2, 1943. Very little blood was shed in the uprising, and it had its elements of comedy. One of the devices of the conspirators was to send chauffeured cars to the homes of the principal armed forces commanders to inform them that there was a coup underway and that they were urgently required at their headquarters—and once these officers were in the cars, to place them under arrest.

As a result of the coup, a new government headed by Major Villarroel and including both members of Radepa and the MNR took power. However, this regime met immediate opposition abroad, particularly from the United States, which succeeded in getting most of the Latin American governments to withhold recognition of the new government.

The reasons for the attitude of the United States government were somewhat complicated. On the one hand, they reflected the fears in the United States that had been aroused by the military coup in Argentina six months earlier on June 4, 1943, which had placed General Pedro Ramírez in the presidency there. The Ramírez government, in which Colonel Juan Perón was the rising star, was frankly pro-Axis in the war then under way. It was feared in Washington that the Argentine military regime was behind the coup in Bolivia that had displaced the friendly General Peñaranda with the unknown Major Villarroel as chief executive. This fear seemed to be confirmed by the almost indecent haste with which the Argentines recognized the new Bolivian government.

Furthermore, there were deep suspicions in the United States of the MNR. It suffered from what has been called elsewhere the "Black Legend"—that it was a pro-Nazi and generally pro-Axis party. These fears were unfounded, although it was true that the MNR was strongly nationalistic and highly critical of the role of the tin-mining companies, in which there were substantial amounts of British and American capital invested. The pro-Axis reputation of the MNR was particularly expounded by the Stalinists and their Bolivian representatives, the PIR.

The role of the PIR in this situation was an equivocal one. Right after the December 2 coup, they "offered" to join the new regime, although setting conditions of their own. It was demanded as the price of their participation that the new government be converted into a "quadripartite" administration in which the Radepa, the MNR, the PIR, and the PIR-controlled Confederación Sindical de Trabajadores Bolivianos would be partners of equal weight.

However, this "offer" was turned down both by the military men and the MNR. The PIR then concluded that the new government was "pro-Nazi." Early in 1944, PIR leader José Antonio Arce was the victim of an assassination attempt of unknown origins in which he was slightly wounded. Soon thereafter he went to the United States, where he inveighed extensively against the Villarroel regime and its supposed pro-Axis proclivities while at the same time teaching at the Communist Thomas Jefferson School in New York City.

The result of the opposition of the United States to the Villarroel government was that the MNR was forced to withdraw from it as the price for gaining recognition from the United States and those Latin American governments that were following its lead. The irony of this situation was that whatever pro-Axis sympathy there was in the new Bolivian regime was to be found among the members of the Radepa, not in the MNR.

Not long after the Villarroel government was recognized by the United States and its allies, the MNR returned to the government. Paz Estenssoro spent much of the next two and a half years as Minister of Finance, and MNR leaders held other important positions in the regime. They had a great deal to do with determining the position of the government on economic and social issues.

ORGANIZATION OF THE MINERS

The Villarroel government brought about very significant changes in Bolivia. One of the most important of these was its encouragement of the organization of the nation's tin miners. The government not only permitted such organization, but gave its strong support to the establishment of what became the country's most important trade union, the Federación Sindical de Trabajadores Mineros (FSTM).

The principal new figure to appear as a leader of the mine workers was Juan Lechín. A veteran of the Chaco War and a well-known soccer player, he had been employed by the Patiño mines on their clerical staff principally to reinforce the strength of the company's soccer team. It is likely that at the time of the December 2, 1943 coup, Lechín was not a member of any political party.

One of the first moves of the Villarroel regime was to make Lechín subprefect of the Siglo XX mining region. This made him the principal government representative in that area. Not long after he had assumed the post, he was visited by a representative of Patiño Mines, who informed him that, as had been the custom, the company would augment his meager salary as subprefect with its own regular contribution. Instead of accepting this with thanks, Lechín is reported to have taken the company representative by the scruff of the neck and the seat of his pants and thrown him out of the office. This action made Lechín a hero immediately with his miner colleagues.

It was apparently about this time that Lechín joined the MNR. In any case, he soon became that party's principal figure within the miners' federation. In 1945, when the FSTM held their congress, Lechín was elected to the highest post in the union, executive secretary, a post which he was to hold for more than 35 years.

At this congress, and for several years thereafter, there were two principal political forces within the miners' federation: the MNR and the POR. At the congress held by the federation in Pulacayo after the fall of the Villarroel government the FSTM adopted a declaration of principles, the Thesis of Pulacayo, which was a more or less orthodox Trotskyist document. Lechín, who was never a political theorist of any note, had entrusted to his Trotskyist friends of the POR, and particularly to Lora, the writing of this fundamental statement of the supposed philosophy of the union. It was to plague him at various times in the future, lending apparent coloration to the claim that he was a Marxist if not a Marxist-Leninist. He was neither.

During the two and a half years of the Villarroel regime, the miners became almost universally unionized. Also during this period, the MNR obtained a solid basis of support among the miners, whose position in national politics became of great strategic importance. Not only were they in a position to cripple the industry that provided most of the country's export income, but through their practice with the use of high explosives, they were able on many occasions to constitute a military force of considerable consequence.

POLICIES TOWARD THE INDIANS

Not only did the Villarroel government encourage the unionization of the miners, but it began to make overtures to the Indian peasants—who constituted the great majority of the population but until then had had little or no role in public affairs. As in the case of the miners, it was the MNR that principally spoke for, elaborated, and carried out the government's policies.

Two actions of major significance were taken with regard to the Indians. First, the institution of *pongaje*, or personal service, was legally abolished. According to this system, Indians living on landowners' holdings were required, in addition to paying part of their crops and working on the fields that the landowner cultivated for his own use, to give periodically a week of free service to the landlord on any kind of project to which he might assign them. According to the decree of the Villarroel government, this kind of personal service could no longer be required of the peasants. Presumably, as long as the Villarroel government remained in power, the decree was more or less enforced. However, unfortunately, during the succeeding conservative administrations, pongaje was restored de facto if not de jure. It was not until the revolution of 1952 that pongaje was finally abolished definitively.

The second action on the part of the Villarroel government was to determine what it was that the Indians themselves wanted. To this end, a National Indian Congress was called about a year before the overthrow of the regime. The president himself attended this session, as did several of his ministers, and there was a long and frank discussion on the grievances of the Indians. Unfortunately, little action was possible to meet some of the grievances before the Villarroel regime was ousted.

For the future, the overtures of the Villarroel government to the Indians were of particular importance insofar as the MNR was concerned. For the first time, these largely middle class political leaders entered into direct contact with representatives of the people who made up the majority of the country's population. The effect was undoubtedly to radicalize the thinking of the MNR leaders concerning the needs of the nation and to lay the groundwork for the fundamental changes that the MNR would make on the behalf of the Indians once it came fully to power.

POLITICS OF THE VILLARROEL REGIME

The principal political forces supporting the Villarroel government were the MNR and the young officers' group of the Radepa. The Trotskyists of the POR, who were, as noted, very active within the miners' federation, also gave critical backing to the regime.

The opposition during these two and a half years consisted not only of the old-line Liberals and various factions of the Republicans, but also of the PIR. The leader of the PIR, José Antonio Arce, ran against Major Villarroel for the presidency in elections that were held during 1944. It was during this election campaign that Arce suffered the attempt on his life. The PIR opposition to the Villarroel government began a long period of cooperation between the Bolivian Stalinists and the defenders of the status quo that was finally to all but destroy the party.

Although opposition parties functioned more or less legally during the Villarroel period, the regime left a good deal to be desired in terms of political democracy. There were frequent arrests of opposition leaders, and there was one notorious incident in which a group of oppositionists, which included General Demetrio Ramos, ex-minister Rubén Terrazas, Senator Luis Calvo, and Carlos Salinas Aramayo, were murdered while under arrest by a group of Army officers. These murders took place during one of these periods in which the MNR was not in the cabinet, and the party certainly did not give its approval to them.

Needless to say, the Villarroel government was strongly opposed by the

Rosca. The regime was a direct challenge to the economic, social, and political domination of the country by the mining interests and rural landlords, and they were unceasing in their denunciation of and plotting against the government.

OVERTHROW OF THE VILLARROEL GOVERNMENT

The Villarroel regime was finally overthrown by a La Paz mob, in which the market women, always a potent influence in the political life of the Bolivian capital, played a major role. While the Army remained in its barracks, the insurrectionists attacked the presidential palace, hauled the president out in front of it, and hanged him on a lamp post right in front of the Palacio Quemado. In future years, when the political tables turned once again, that lamp post was to become a sort of national shrine, with a plaque in front of it explaining the tragedy of July 21, 1946, and a soldier always standing at attention before it.

Perhaps because of his martyrdom, Major Villarroel came to have a very special place in the hagiography of Bolivian politics. The honoring of the place of his martyrdom began during the government of the MNR, but was continued by all of the anti-MNR governments that held office after 1964. The military men who dominated those governments might have been united on little else, but they were united in regarding themselves as heirs of Major Villarroel. He joined another supposed martyr, Colonel Busch, in being regarded as a kind of patron saint of modern Bolivia. A favorite way of showing this came to be posters that upon appropriate occasions would be put up throughout the country with the incumbent military ruler against a shadowy background showing the busts of Colonel Busch and Major Villarroel.

THE POST-VILLARROEL REGIME

With the overthrow of the Villarroel government, a so-called revolutionary junta of military men and civilians came to power. Its basic job was to establish the status quo ante through the mechanism of elections held under the same limited franchise that had prevailed before the advent of the Villarroel government.

There were two presidential candidates in the elections. The various factions of the Republican Party supported Enrique Hertzog, while the Liberal Party named Tomás Manuel de Elio, who ran with the backing of the PIR. Hertzog was the victor.

Understandably, the MNR was unable to run a presidential candidate in this election. However, indirectly, it did have nominees for Congress. For the purpose of the election, what was called the Miners Bloc was organized. Drawing its support mainly from the mining areas, it presented lists of candidates for both senator and deputy. These candidates were drawn from both the MNR and the Trotskyist POR. Two senators, Juan Lechín of the MNR, and Lucio Mendivil of the POR, were elected, as were half a dozen deputies, including POR leader Lora.

The members of the Miners Bloc served only fitfully in Congress. Not many months had passed before Senator Lechín was arrested under charges of seditious activities against the regime. He was deported, and from then until the revolution of 1952, Lechín and other members of the bloc spent longer or shorter periods in exile, interspersed with periods of clandestine residence and underground activity inside of Bolivia. Lechín was in hiding in La Paz at the time that he was one of the principal organizers and leaders of the April 1952 revolution.

Meanwhile, the government remained from 1947 until May 1951 in the hands of a constitutional and civilian, albeit very conservative, administration. However, in October 1949, President Hertzog, pleading ill-health, resigned and turned the government over to his vice-president, Mamerto Urriolagoitia. Both were representatives of the Partido de Unificación Republicana Socialista (PURS), which had been established shortly after the overthrow of President Villarroel to bring together all of the factions of the much-splintered traditional Republican Party.

DECLINE OF THE PIR

The 1946–51 period was the last in which the government of Bolivia was clearly in the hands of the Rosca. Although officially an administration of the PURS, during part of the time it had within the cabinet members of the Liberal Party as well. Certainly, the PURS and the Liberals were united in their violent opposition to the MNR and all elements that had been associated with the Villarroel regime.

Unity of the parties of the Rosca was not surprising. What *was* surprising, perhaps, was that during most of the 1946–51 period the pro-Stalinist PIR also cooperated with the regime. With the election of a new Congress early in 1947, José Antonio Arce was chosen to preside over the Chamber of Deputies. During about half of what the MNR people came to call the Sexenio (1946–52), the PIR also had members of the cabinet, including part of this time the Minister of Labor.

This collaboration with the Rosca governments of the Sexenio was virtually fatal for the PIR. It utterly destroyed the party's influence in the organized labor movement, with the result that most of the leaders of the railway workers, industrial workers, chauffeurs, and other unions that had traditionally been members of the PIR ended the period as members of the MNR.

The pro-Rosca attitude of the PIR also led to a major split in the party. In 1950 most of the leaders of the youth wing of the PIR withdrew to constitute a new Communist Party of Bolivia. This new group quite obviously had the blessing of the leaders of the world Communist movement, and with the overthrow of the Rosca regime it emerged as a clear-cut Stalinist Communist Party.

The PIR was thus reduced to a handful of intellectuals. After the Sexenio, the principal position of leadership was held by Ricardo Anaya. The party emerged from the Sexenio as a very minor political party. It still continues to exist, but for the last 30 years has had no significant role in national politics.

THE MNR STRUGGLE AGAINST THE REGIME OF THE SEXENIO

The party that made the largest gains during the Sexenio was the MNR. It carried the brunt of the struggle against the incumbent regime, and in doing so rallied behind it virtually all of the working class and a large part of the country's middle class as well.

The struggle of the MNR was bitter and occasionally violent. Immediately upon the fall of the Villarroel regime, virtually all of the nonlabor leaders of the party were exiled. During the Sexenio, Víctor Paz Estenssoro made no effort to come back into the country. However, many of the party's other leaders did come back, including not only Lechín, but Hernán Siles and various others who had played a significant role in the Busch and Villarroel governments.

It was during the Sexenio that the MNR came to dominate without any question the organized labor movement. Not only did it solidify its position in the tin-mining unions, gaining there largely at the expense of the Trotskyists, but it also gained ascendancy over virtually all of the unions in La Paz and the other major cities, the great majority of which formerly had been controlled by the PIR. About the only union group of any significance that remained outside the control of the MNR was the small organization of anarchist-controlled labor groups, the Federación Obrera Local of La Paz, which was made up principally of artisans' organizations.

There is no doubt that the MNR itself was radicalized during the Sexenio. Although it had since its inception been strongly opposed to the influence of the "big three" mining companies over the country's economic and political life, it had until 1946 only supported modest moves—such as the foreign exchange decree of 1939—to limit that influence. Now, however, the party leaders became firmly convinced that so long as Patiño, Aramayo, and Hochschild continued to dominate the nation's principal source of foreign exchange, no fundamental changes in the country's institutions would be possible. Therefore, the MNR emerged from the Sexenio strongly committed to the nationalization of the "big three" mining firms.

Similarly, in the period before 1946, the MNR leaders had been committed to do something on behalf of the Indian majority of the population. However, they had been only vaguely aware of just what it was they wanted to do. During the Sexenio, their thinking advanced markedly on this subject, as it did with regard to the mining industry. The MNR leaders became convinced that the most fundamental and necessary action to be done for the Indians was to give them back the land. Therefore, the party emerged from the Sexenio firmly committed to carrying out a drastic agrarian reform.

The years in exile served to put the MNR leaders in closer contact with reformist political movements in other countries. It perhaps also gave them a chance to think more clearly about their own ideology. The upshot was that in their own minds they came to associate their party with National Revolutionary parties of the Democratic Left that existed in other Latin American countries, such as the Aprista Party of Peru, Democratic Action in Venezuela, and the Mexican government party known by then as the Partido Revolucionario Institucional.

In their struggle with the regimes of the Sexenio, the MNR used virtually all weapons available to them. They led strikes of different groups of workers and in 1950 a general strike against the regime. In August 1949 they led a full-fledged insurrection that held control of the departments of Santa Cruz and Cochabamba for several days, but was not able to extend beyond there and in the end was defeated.

THE ELECTION OF 1951

With the approach of the end of the Hertzog-Urriolagoitia term of office, elections for a new president and congress were called in May 1951. There were six presidential nominees in these elections. President Urriolagoitia threw his support behind the candidate of the PURS, Gabriel Gosalávez, the Bolivian ambassador in Buenos Aires, who also enjoyed the backing of the small Partido Social Democrático. The Aramayo mining interests backed Guillermo Gutiérrez Vea-Murguía, editor of *La Razón*, the La Paz daily newspaper owned by Carlos Aramayo. Tomás Manuel de Elio was again the candidate of the Liberal Party, as was José Antonio Arce of the PIR. The Falange Socialista Boliviana supported General Bernardino Bilbao Rioja.

There was considerable debate within the MNR about whether it should try to participate in this election at all, even though the government made it clear that it would be allowed to name candidates. The final decision was that the party should participate, and so Víctor Paz Estenssoro was named for the presidency and Hernán Siles for the vice-presidency, and a list of congressional nominees was also presented. The MNR candidates were backed in this election by the POR and by the new Partido Comunista.

When the votes were counted in the May 1951 election, it was clear that the MNR candidates for president and vice-president had at least a plurality. The government maintained that they had not received the 51 percent that was required by the constitution, and, therefore, the decision between Paz Estenssoro and Gosalávez, the two front runners, would have to be made by the newly elected Congress. A year later, after they had seized power, the MNR leaders claimed that they had discovered the 1951 ballots in the presidential palace, had counted them, and they showed that the MNR had gotten more than three-fourths of the votes.

President Urriolagoitia did not want to run any risk that the MNR nominees might win. He summoned the principal leaders of the armed forces and told them that he intended to turn the government over to them, rather than to allow the MNR to be victorious. Thereupon, there was extensive consultation among the military, and they finally agreed to assume power through a military junta when and if President Urriolagoitia resigned, which he promptly did. Under no circumstances, the military chiefs decided, should the MNR be permitted to come to power.

The upshot was that a new Military Junta government, headed by General José Ballivián, the Army commander, assumed power in May 1951. Upon taking office, the Junta promised that its principal function would be that of arranging for new elections. However, by the time that it was ousted almost eleven months later, the Junta Militar had taken no concrete steps to this end. They had come to enjoy the exercise and fruits of power.

Probably the major achievement of the military government of 1951-52 was its arrangement for the sending to Bolivia by the United Nations of an economic survey group, known as the Keenleyside Mission after its Canadian chief, to study Bolivia's potential for economic development. Although the mission expressed certain reservations about the negative effects that the country's political and administrative instability had on economic development prospects, it did recommend the sending to Bolivia of an expanded U.N. group, to work closely with various parts of the Bolivian government on drawing up and carrying out a more detailed program of economic development. That mission headed by a Columbia University professor, Carter Goodrich, had just arrived in Bolivia a day or two before the overthrow of the Ballivián government.

CONCLUSION

Obviously, the installation of a new military government was only a stop-gap measure to preserve the rule of the Rosca. The Ballivián regime had no program other than that of preventing the ascension to power of the Movimiento Nacionalista Revolucionario. It suggested no reforms designed to limit the power of the Rosca, establish a basis for political democracy, or right the age-old injustices suffered by the Indian peasants and by the miners. Indeed, it could not have been expected to do so, since it had originally been installed in power by the Rosca. Perhaps the most surprising thing about the Ballivián regime was not that it was overthrown after only 11 months, but that it lasted so long.

6

REVOLUTIONARY BOLIVIA

On April 9, 1952, there began in Bolivia one of the major Latin American revolutions of the twentieth century. In some ways it reversed the course of Bolivian history since the coming of the Spanish conquistadores early in the sixteenth century. In another way it failed in its efforts to alter fundamentally the country's traditional political patterns.

THE INSURRECTION

The uprising that began in La Paz and other cities and in the mining camps on April 9, 1952, was directed by Hernán Siles, who had been chosen vice-president in the abortive election of 1951, and Juan Lechín, the head of the Mineworkers' Federation. It was a joint effort of the MNR and the Carabineros, the militarized national police, and the man who was at first destined to be placed in the presidential palace by the revolutionaries was General Antonio Selemé, the commander of the Carabineros.

The fighting was fierce in the capital city. Most of the military units stationed there remained loyal to the incumbent regime, and there was widespread street fighting between armed civilians recruited by the MNR, and Carabinero units on the one side and Army formations on the other.

At one point, when the situation in La Paz seemed to be turning against the revolution, Siles and Lechín told General Selemé that it would be advisable for him to seek refuge in an embassy because if the uprising failed and he was captured, his life might well be in danger. As a result, the Carabineros commander fled to the embassy of Chile.

Meanwhile, however, the revolution had been a success elsewhere in the country, particularly in the mining centers. The tin miners used their dynamite to very good effect and captured control not only of the mining camps, but of the nearby cities as well. By the end of the second day, contingents of miners had arrived around La Paz and were threatening to move down into the city. They guaranteed the triumph of the revolt in the capital.

With the victory of the revolution, General Selemé left his embassy refuge and came out to claim his place at the head of the new government to be formed by the revolutionaries. However, he was politely but firmly informed by Lechín and Siles that since he had fled the scene when the situation appeared most hopeless he had forfeited all claims to be leader of the new government. The best that he could salvage from the situation was the post of ambassador to Chile.

Instead of installing the Carabineros' commander as the new president, the victorious revolutionaries under the leadership of Siles and Lechín set about to recognize the results of the presidential election of 1951. They proclaimed Víctor Paz Estenssoro to be the constitutional president of the republic and Hernán Siles to be the new vice-president. With this move, control of the government was firmly in the hands of the MNR.

FIRST MOVES OF THE REVOLUTIONARY REGIME

Soon after the return of Paz Estenssoro from his exile in Buenos Aires, the new government began to lay the groundwork for profound changes in the country's economy, society, and polity. One of their very first moves was to issue a new electoral law, providing for universal adult suffrage, thus extending the franchise to the great mass of the illiterate Indian peasantry as well as to other citizens who were unable to read and write, as had been required of voters theretofore.

The revolutionary government also presaged other profound changes. It established a new Ministry of Peasant Affairs, which was to play a crucial role in the transformations of the subsequent years. It established a commission to draw up a law nationalizing the country's large mining enterprises and also established a commission to write an agrarian reform law. Finally, the revolutionary regime announced that there would henceforward be a system of "co-government," in which the partners would be the MNR party and the organized labor movement. To exercise the labor side of this agreement, there was quickly organized a new central labor organization, the Central Obrera Boliviana (COB), of which Lechín became the executive secretary.

Although the MNR's control over the government was virtually unchallenged during the early months of the revolutionary regime, the new leaders took steps to make sure that this would continue to be the case. To this end, they officially dissolved the country's armed forces, sending their officers and men home and proclaiming that henceforth the government would depend for its military support on the armed militia of the workers and peasants unions. For about a year and a half, Bolivia did not possess a regular army, navy, or air force. However, the Carabineros were left intact, in recognition of the role they had played in the victory of the revolution.

THE NATIONALIZATION OF THE MINES

One of the most urgent items on the agenda of the revolutionary government was the nationalization of the "big three" tin mines belonging to the Patiño, Aramayo, and Hochschild companies. Indeed, in retrospect, it is clear that the government, although appearing to move quickly, in fact moved entirely too slowly on the mine nationalization issue.

A commission in which the Mine Workers' Federation participated drew up the new law nationalizing the mines. It was then submitted to public debate, particularly by the COB. However, it was not finally enacted until October 1952.

The new decree-law provided that the mines and all other property belonging to the "big three" companies would be taken over by the government. To run the new nationalized mining industry, the Corporación Minera de Bolivia (COMIBOL) was established. It was provided that the companies would ultimately be compensated for the property that had been taken from them, but the exact details of such compensation were to be worked out later and were not provided for in the law.

A unique system was set up for the administration of the mines under COMIBOL. This was the "control obrero" (labor control). According to this system, union officials were designated at each level in the COMIBOL who had a veto power over the operations of the managers, and there was representation of the Federación Sindical de Trabajadores Mineros at the top level of the COMIBOL.

The upshot of the control obrero system, together with the general euphoria that accompanied the revolution, was the utter disintegration of labor discipline in the mines. The management personnel was subject to irresistible pressure on the part of the designated union officials, and in many instances where the management people attempted to resist this pressure, they were summarily fired by the control obrero.

The management difficulties of the new firm were greatly complicated by the fact that the old mining companies did everything within their power to sabotage the operations of the COMIBOL. They offered jobs outside of Bolivia to management and technical personnel, and threatened those who would not accept these jobs that they would lose all of their retirement and pension rights with the companies. As a result, almost all of the foreign management personnel, and many Bolivians as well, not only left the Bolivian mining industry, but left the country also. Furthermore, the mining companies had their retiring officials take with them virtually all of the geological maps that the companies possessed—and for some strange reason they were not prevented from doing so. Finally, the tin companies were successful for some time in bringing pressure on the United States government so that it would not adopt a friendly attitude toward the MNR government.

The upshot of all of this was an economic crisis in the mining industry. Output of COMIBOL declined for almost a decade. Costs of production increased, in part as a result of management problems and in part because of the rehiring of substantial numbers of workers who had been laid off because of labor and political disputes during the Sexenio. In addition, tin prices sagged during some of the period. The economic benefits that the revolutionary leaders had hoped would result from government ownership of the mines were very slow in coming.

As time went on, there developed a genuine conflict of interest between the miners and the revolutionary government. The miners, understandably enough, were interested in getting as much out of the nationalization for themselves as possible, whereas the revolutionary government was anxious to use the resources from the mining industry for the development of other aspects of the economy and for various other programs that it soon got under way.

The first serious showdown between the mine leaders and the MNR government came early in the Siles administration in 1957, when the Siles government adopted a "stabilization" program that was designed to curb the runaway inflation to which the economy was by that time subjected. One aspect of this program was a limitation of the operation of the commissaries that functioned in the mining camps. During the first five years of the revolutionary government the prices in these commissaries were held at very low levels in the face of massive inflation in the rest of the economy; so it became the custom for the miners to buy large quantities of goods at the commissaries and resell much of what they bought to other elements of the population at a substantial profit. It was reported that miners were making a great deal more income from their commissary privileges than they were from their wages. Naturally, they did not want any interference with such a system.

After first endorsing the stabilization program, Lechín became its most vocal opponent. He retreated to the mining communities at one point to lead a general strike against the Siles government, in an attempt to get it to give up the stabilization program. However, President Siles made a personal trip to several of the mining camps—in the face of threats that he would be murdered if he went to any of them—and succeeded in convincing the lower ranking mining leaders to call off the walkout.

Subsequently, during the second administration of President Paz Estenssoro, there was another bitter dispute, this time over the so-called Triangular Plan to reorganize the mining industry. Among other things, it again involved restricting the commissaries, where the old practices had tended to return, and it provided for rationalization of the industry, closing down unproductive mines and concentrating investments on those that still were able to produce substantial amounts of tin. Although there was no showdown over this issue such as had occurred in 1957, the final factor in alienating the miners from the revolutionary government was the decision of President Paz Estenssoro to run for a third term, thus passing over Lechín, his vice-president, who had been promised the MNR nomination for 1964. As a result, Lechín and the miners' federation first split the MNR and organized their own party, and then supported the overthrow of the MNR regime in November 1964.

PREPARATIONS FOR THE AGRARIAN REFORM

Although the nationalization of the mines was dramatic and perhaps received more attention abroad than anything else then going on in the country, the agrarian reform was much more significant in a long-term sense. It in effect gave the land back to the Indians.

It has been argued by many writers that the government of the MNR was forced into the agrarian reform because of land seizures by peasants in the Cochabamba Valley and elsewhere. However, this is a complete misunderstanding of the situation.

At the time it seized power, the MNR was thoroughly committed to a redistribution of the country's landholdings. However, before this measure could be taken, it was necessary to prepare the ground for it. This is what the government did during the first 15 months it was in power.

The key to this operation was the Ministry of Peasant Affairs, a unique kind of government organization. Its province was anything that had to do with the peasants and their welfare. Cutting across the jurisdictions of such ministries as those of education, agriculture, and health, it undertook completely new kinds of activities that had not been considered by any part of the government until that time.

The government and the Ministry of Peasant Affairs had three fundamental tasks to accomplish during the first year of the revolutionary government. One was to draft the new agrarian reform law, the second was to organize the peasants, and the third was to expand vastly the social services available to the peasants.

The drafting of the agrarian reform law was not directly the province of the Ministry of Peasant Affairs, although it was involved in the process. A special commission, headed by Vice-President Siles and containing representatives of various labor organizations, political parties, and the peasant groups and the Ministry of Peasant Affairs, undertook this task. They brought in experts from Mexico, which had undergone a fundamental agrarian reform as part of its revolution, to give them advice on the matter. This advice, in part at least, was that the Bolivians should not adopt any hard and fast agrarian reform institution such as the communal farm, or *ejido*, that had been established in Mexico, but should leave the peasants free to decide how they wanted to organize the land that was to be turned over to them.

The proposed agrarian reform law, once adopted by the commission, was again submitted for public discussion, particularly by the COB. Representatives of three different political groups spoke at the debate that took place in the COB. The speaker representing the Communist Party proposed what Lechín (who was there representing not only the COB leadership but the MNR as well) commented was a translation of the Chinese Communist agrarian reform law. The Trotskyist party leader who also spoke opposed the idea of setting up a petty-bourgeois peasantry as a result of the reform, as was being proposed by the Agrarian Reform Commission. Lechín, who spoke for his party, gave a strong defense of the government's measure and clearly had the support of the majority of those present, most of whom were MNR members.

However, even more significant than the drafting of a land redistribution law was the work of the Ministry of Peasant Affairs in organizing the peasantry. Up to that point in most of the highlands and in the Yungas, the Indians had been an inert body without formal organizations to speak for them, and it was necessary before the agrarian reform process began to have established peasant organizations that could cooperate with the governmental authorities in asking for the land and helping to decide the basis upon which it should be distributed.

The ministry, in effect, organized three different kinds of groups among the Indians, groups that were sometimes almost indistinguishable from one another. These were peasant unions, militia units, and local branches of the MNR.

The peasant unions were a key element in the proposed land reform. They had to guide the governmental authorities in deciding which land should be expropriated, who was entitled (in accordance with the law) to receive land, and how the land should be organized once it had been turned over to the peasants. Furthermore, pending the enactment of the new law, their role was to carry on "collective bargaining" with the landlords concerning the conditions under which the land would be rented to their members. All rent was in any case to be in terms of cash, since the prevalent semifeudal sharecropping system was outlawed immediately upon the triumph of the revolution.

The militia units were also essential to the revolution. The arms taken from the dissolved armed forces were in large part turned over to the peasant militia units. The immediate task of the militiamen was to thwart any attempt by the landlords to resist the reforms under way, and their long run purpose was to defend the revolutionary government itself. Certainly during the last eight years of the MNR regime, its major military support came from the peasant militia; and it was only after the leaders of the reestablished army became convinced that the militia were no longer efficient military units that they dared to move against the revolutionary government. The local units of the MNR were almost indistinguishable from the peasant unions. However, during the MNR regime their task was to organize political support for the regime, at election time and in between elections.

Finally, the Ministry of Peasant Affairs had the task of beginning to extend to the peasants myriad services that had for long been more or less available to the people in the cities, but not to the peasantry. Most important in this regard were schools and health services. The ministry undertook to establish a network of primary schools in the rural areas, where very few had existed before. The Indians' response to this was overwhelming, and the ministry was hard put to find enough people to teach in the new schools that in many cases the Indians built themselves. Often it was necessary to use miners and other Indians who somehow had succeeded in obtaining at least a primary school education to impart at least a few years of education to the Indian children.

The ministry also undertook to organize at least primitive health facilities in the countryside. Often these were little more than first aid stations or centers where injections and other basic health services could be provided. Here, too, the ministry was virtually overwhelmed by the eagerness of the peasants to see even the most rudimentary health facilities established in their villages.

THE AGRARIAN REFORM

On August 2, 1953 the Agrarian Reform Law was finally proclaimed at a ceremony at Ucureña in the Cochabamba Valley by President Paz Estenssoro. It provided for massive transfer of rural property, particularly in the Altiplano and the Yungas, from the white or near-white traditional landowners to the Indian peasants. In the case of estates that had been cultivated by "semifeudal" methods, as defined in the law—sharecropping, virtually no use of machinery, no application of scientific agricultural methods—the total estate was taken over by the government. In the case of estates that had been cultivated by "modern" methods of wage labor, machinery, and more or less use of scientific technology, a top limit was established and all land in excess of that limit was given to the peasants.

The peasants were proclaimed immediately the owners of any pieces of land that their landlords had allowed them to use for their huts or to produce crops for themselves (or even for sale). The law also provided for a procedure for the ultimate transfer of all or part of the rest of the estate (in accordance with how it had been previously cultivated) to the peasants, after land surveys and decisions on who had the right to receive the land had been made.

A hierarchy was established defining who had the right to the land that was to be redistributed. Those peasants currently living on and working the land had the first claim. Behind them were peasants who had formerly lived on the estate involved. There was also certain preference for veterans of the Chaco War, and finally, any other peasant who could demonstrate that he was willing and able to use the land was entitled to receive some if there was enough available on a particular estate.

There was also provision in the law for compensating the former land-owners. However, they were to be compensated in government bonds drawing modest interest that were to run for 20 years. The amount of compensation they were to receive was to be based on the value that they had previously declared the land to have for tax purposes.

As a matter of actual fact, few landlords bothered to collect their compensation. Due to their own past behavior, the value of the land was grossly under-stated, and in any case, by the time they could have collected their compensation bonds, the runaway inflation was well under way and the bonds were quite literally not worth much more than the paper they were printed on.

The upshot of the law was that the Indian peasants immediately became owners of plots of varying sizes. Over the succeeding years, the process of sub-dividing the rest of the estates went forward, hampered by a lack of personnel qualified to do the surveying and demarcation that was required for the process. However, by the end of the MNR regime, the overwhelming majority of the land in the Altiplano and the valleys had been turned over to the Indian peasants.

There were undoubtedly many cases in which the land was effectively turned over to the Indians long before the legal processes had been carried out. Many landowners abandoned their lands and went to live in the cities or, if they could afford it, abroad. In some instances, they were in fact run off of their estates by the Indians. However, the attitude of the peasants toward their land-owners varied greatly, depending in large part on what the relations between them had been before the revolution.

The Indians were left free to decide how they would cultivate the land they received. Although the MNR government encouraged the formation of co-operatives for specific purposes, such as for purchasing inputs and selling pro-duce, it had no preconceived notions on how the land should be organized. As a matter of practice, in the overwhelming majority of cases the peasants divided the land among the various heads of families of the community and cultivated it on a family basis.

INCOMPLETENESS OF THE AGRARIAN REFORM

Land redistribution was a necessary but not sufficient requirement for re-habilitation of the Indians and their incorporation into the wider economy and political life of the country. Although the agrarian reform gave the peasants a kind of security and a status as small property owners that they had not had since the Spanish conquest, much more was required for them to become more productive farmers, and before the great gap separating the Indian peasant from the mestizo and near-white city dweller could be bridged and both parts of the population could be merged into a single Bolivian nation.

On the economic level, the new Indian landowner needed credit, technical assistance and an extension service, help with getting his products to market, and a variety of other inputs to convert his operation from subsistence farming into commercial agriculture. On a cultural level, it would have been wise to have built—in the initial enthusiasm of the peasants to build schools—an educational network throughout the rural parts of the country. Such schools would not only have helped the process of breaking down cultural barriers between the peasants and the city folk by making the youngsters bilingual, but would also have given them training in how to be farmers.

The kind of effort which, if it had become universalized on the Altiplano and in the Yungas, would have vastly increased the productivity and levels of living of the peasants and at the same time helped to break down their isolation from non-Indian Bolivia was shown by a young professor who spent two years in Bolivia in the late 1960s and early 1970s. Lane Vanderslice spent about $2,000 a year on his own Point Four program during his residence in the country. Among other things, he helped establish local stores in seven Indian villages, lending small amounts to Indians who were ready to undertake such an effort. In another project, he worked with two villages, to help the Indians there to use simple kinds of fertilizer in growing their traditional crop, potatoes. At first convincing seven or eight of the more adventurous members of these communities to experiment with the fertilizer, he finally convinced virtually all of them to use it for at least part of their crop when it became clear that the effect of such use was to increase output many times over.

Of course, these projects were "unspectacular" except for the Indian communities involved. They required Vanderslice to get to know and gain the confidence of the villagers, who were naturally suspicious of a gringo from the city. The projects involved working with the Indians under rather primitive conditions, combining patience with a willingness to get his hands dirty alongside those he was trying to help.

Unfortunately, neither the MNR governments nor their successors ever undertook this kind of program on a large scale. Probably the only administration that made at least a beginning in establishing—with the help of the United States Agency for International Development (AID)—the kind of agricultural extension service and credit facility that might have been the basis of an economic and cultural reorientation of the Indian peasants was that of General René Barrientos (1966-69). He spoke Quechua, and had a deep interest in trying to help the Indians to become better farmers and grazers and to further the integration of the two sectors of Bolivian society.

Other governments did not institute such programs nor see the need for them. The MNR administrations gave highest priority to completing the work of land redistribution. They were assured—or thought they were—of the political and military loyalty of the Indian masses, and found the problems of the mines and of high politics to have priority over the much more mundane day-to-day work with the peasantry.

Nor did the far leftist groups that often professed to speak on behalf of the Indians see their way clear to doing anything practical to help them. The university students, whose far Left inclinations were particularly notable, found it much more interesting to have political strikes, demonstrations in the capital city, and auto-da-fé burnings of hapless automobiles in front of the university skyscraper in La Paz than to go out in the countryside to dirty their hands in practical work to help the Indians improve their situation and status.

In spite of its incompleteness, the agrarian reform carried out by the MNR revolutionary governments brought profound transformations to the countryside. Possession of the land in the highlands and the valleys gave the Indians a political power that they had not possessed since Inca times. For the most part, they have used this power passively, being willing to tolerate any government in La Paz that would leave them in control of their land. Needless to say, no government of the MNR or afterward made any move to dispossess them.

Slowly, as a result of economic rather than political forces, the Indians have during the last three decades come increasingly to be part of the market economy. The immediate impact of the agrarian reform was to bring the peasants to grow more food for their own consumption and less for sale to the cities. Slowly increasing awareness of the items that can be bought with money—transistor radios stand high in their estimation in this regard—has brought the Indians to offer increasing amounts of their products to the market.

The growing commercialization of Indian agriculture has brought into existence different kinds of middlemen, most of them drawn from the Indian community itself. Principal among these have been truck owners who have gone out in the countryside to purchase the goods that the Indians have had for sale. Although these people have been mainly Indians, they have often been the source of bitter complaint on the part of members of the Indian communities. They have been accused of purchasing cheaply and selling dearly, the Indians often not being in a position to bargain effectively, faced as they have been with the need to get goods to market and not having the facilities to deliver goods themselves. However, increasingly large numbers of Indian villagers have been buying their own trucks on a cooperative basis to free themselves from dependence on these entrepreneurs.

Another kind of "intermediary" who has grown up among the Bolivian Indians since the 1952 revolution is the political *cacique*. These local leaders originated as heads of the peasant unions and units of the MNR that were established during the first years of the revolution. With the disintegration of the MNR on a national basis, particularly after the overthrow of the Paz Estenssoro government in 1964, these leaders came to be largely local bosses serving as spokesmen for their constituents before succeeding governments and at the same time often providing real support to these governments or (more often) the appearance of such support. Given the refusal of all governments since 1964 to allow the MNR or any other party to maintain an integrated party network in the countryside, the caciques, although very important in any given locality, have had only very limited impact on national political events.

The problem of bringing modern education to the Indians has proved a long and difficult one to solve. Illiteracy is still quite high among them. They remain relatively isolated from the urban society, and continue predominantly to speak their Quechua and Aymara languages. Their slowness in integrating into the "national" society is borne witness to by the fact that although caciques are of great importance on a local level, few Indians have achieved posts in parliament—when that institution has functioned—and only a handful of them have achieved anything like a position of national leadership.

The Bolivian Indian in the 1980s is undoubtedly much more aware of the "outside world" than he was in the 1950s. The development of highways has facilitated his occasional visits to the urban centers or to other Indian villages. The radio—particularly the transistor—has made it possible for him to hear programs in his own language, originating in Bolivia or in neighboring Peru, as well as those beamed from afar by the Cubans, Russians, and others eager to exert influence in the High Andes. Thus, even the illiterate Indian knows much more about what is happening in his own country and with its neighbors and faraway countries (the existence of which he was not previously aware) than was once the case. However, for the most part, this new knowledge has not moved him to break out of the self-imposed isolation that was for centuries his defense against the encroachment of the Spanish conquerors and their heirs.

ECONOMIC DEVELOPMENT OF THE REVOLUTIONARY GOVERNMENT

A third major thrust of the revolutionary government of the MNR was that of economic development. It laid particular stress on three things: expansion of the oil industry, road building, and opening up the eastern part of the country.

The first effort of the MNR government in the oil industry was to make the government firm YPFB more productive. During the first couple of years of the regime, substantial sums were spent on obtaining equipment necessary to expand YPFB production, and the results were quite positive, the firm soon becoming able to provide all of the country's petroleum needs.

The MNR government leaders were anxious to develop petroleum as a complement to mining products as a national export. Largely due to advice from AID and high officials of the Eisenhower administration, they rewrote the country's basic oil code to permit foreign oil companies once again to obtain concessions in Bolivia. During the Siles administration in the late 1950s, there was extensive prospecting by a considerable number of foreign firms, principally from the United States. However, it was the Gulf Oil Corporation that had most success in these explorations and became the principal foreign oil firm functioning in the country. It also built a pipeline to the coast, to permit Bolivian oil to be exported through a Chilean port.

However, the great hopes that the MNR leaders had that Bolivia might become a major oil exporter did not bear fruit. Its shipments of petroleum have never come to be a significant force in the world market. More success, however, met the efforts to become an exporter of natural gas, and both Argentina and Brazil came to depend substantially on Bolivian exports of this product.

Road building was of major importance to the revolutionary government. In the Altiplano it served to make contact with the far Indian communities possible and to facilitate both the agrarian reform and the mobilization of the Indians in support of the regime as well as aid in making possible the modest educational and health programs that the government mounted for the peasants. Road building also served to unify the national market, thus aiding both commercial agriculture and manufacturing. With the help of the AID, a large semi-autonomous government enterprise was established both to expand the highway network and maintain roads already constructed in the highlands.

However, the major accomplishment of the revolutionary government in road building was undoubtedly the Cochabamba-Santa Cruz Highway, a project begun many years before the ascent of the MNR to power. However, it had made very slow progress until Paz Estenssoro became president. Within little more than a year thereafter, a substantial dirt highway had been completed between these two cities, one in the Valley of Cochabamba and the other the capital of the most promising of the eastern departments of the country.

This Cochabamba-Santa Cruz Highway became the basis for the efforts to expand the economy of the eastern part of the country. These efforts included major attempts to get people from the frequently overpopulated valleys and parts of the highlands to move to the east, and also involved the development of new economic activities in Santa Cruz and nearby departments.

Feeder roads were built off of the Cochabamba-Santa Cruz Highway, and encouragement was given to people to settle along these as well as along the main highway itself. In Santa Cruz, the government invested directly in a number of enterprises, most notably the sugar industry. However, even more important, particularly after the fall of the revolutionary government, was the stimulation that the highway provided for private entrepreneurs to go into the Santa Cruz region. That region became the center of tropical and semitropical commercial agriculture in which relatively large landholdings and peasant proprietors both participated.

Attention was paid also to the mineral resources of the Santa Cruz region. Aside from the petroleum industry, which was located there, the most important of these resources was iron ore along the Brazilian frontier. Although the opening up of those iron ore reserves never got beyond the exploration stage during the revolutionary government, it was largely the efforts of the MNR regime in stimulating the overall economy of the region that made the exploitation of iron ore a practical possibility.

OUTSIDE AID TO ECONOMIC DEVELOPMENT

In its economic development efforts, the revolutionary regime received significant help from two sources, the United Nations and the United States. Almost coincidental with the April 1952 uprising there had arrived in Bolivia a UN technical mission, headed by Carter Goodrich, an American economist. Although there were debates within the new MNR government as to whether this mission would be allowed to stay in the country, Goodrich had fortunately established good personal relations with Siles even before April 9, and it was finally decided that Goodrich and his associates would be allowed to continue in Bolivia to carry out the mission that had brought them there.

A unique relationship was worked out by Goodrich and the leaders of the new government. It was decided that the members of the UN group, all of whom were technicians of one kind or another from several different countries, would be integrated into the appropriate parts of the Bolivian government to advise, train, and administer improvement in the functioning of various social and economic branches of the Bolivian government. Although it would be extremely hard to quantify to results of the United Nations Technical Mission, it was certainly a unique experiment in technical aid by a group of UN experts.

Other UN help came from the Economic Commission for Latin America (ECLA), with its headquarters in Santiago, Chile. ECLA sent in a mission, headed by José Antonio Mayobre, a leading Venezuelan economist, to make an extensive survey of the Bolivian economy. Its report was certainly the most complete overall view of the state of Bolivia's economy that had been made up to that point, and undoubtedly was of considerable help to the economic planners and administrators of the revolutionary government.

Finally, a number of the other international agencies associated with the United Nations also gave various kinds of technical aid and advice. These included, among others, the International Labor Organization, the Food and Agricultural Organization, and the United Nations Educational, Scientific, and Cultural Organization.

Whereas the United Nations gave principally technical advice and help, and attempted to stay out of political matters, the United States, after hesitation, gave both technical advice and very extensive financial support, becoming very much involved in Bolivian politics. However, this did not commence until more than a year after the MNR came to power.

There was considerable hesitation on the part of the U.S. government—under Truman and Eisenhower—to extend aid to a regime as frankly revolutionary as that of the MNR. There was absolutely no willingness to do so until some preliminary arrangement concerning compensation for the expropriated tin-mining companies had been made.

Only half jokingly, the author has frequently argued that the key to the fact that the United States finally gave as extensive economic aid to the Bolivian revolutionary government as it did was, in large part, the high altitude of La Paz. The 12,000 feet above sea-level location of the Bolivian capital meant that no rich businessman or other political appointee of any American president would ever seek to fill the post of ambassador there. Hence, the country was fortunate in having a series of professional diplomats assigned to La Paz as U.S. ambassador, most of whom had sympathy for what the Bolivian revolutionary leaders were trying to do.

The actual process of agreement to aid Bolivia began with the trip to the country of Milton Eisenhower, the president's brother, in mid-1953. He was apparently impressed with the sincerity of the desire of the MNR leaders to transform their country, and was also convinced that they were not "Communists." It was upon his recommendation—after a preliminary agreement of the Paz Estenssoro government to pay a part of the income from tin exports to the expropriated companies pending ultimate decision of how much they should be paid overall—that the United States finally began its aid program to Bolivia.

This aid program was very varied. It included help for road construction and maintenance, agricultural development, and technical advice in a great variety of different fields. It also included what was then an unusual kind of aid: general budget support to help cover the very substantial deficits of the Bolivian government. Some of the U.S. diplomats and technicians developed close personal relations with Bolivian counterparts and with the country's political leaders. Upon occasion, they were even quite free to give them political advice; which in view of, on the one hand, the importance of U.S. aid and, on the other, the clear sympathy of the U.S. officials for the revolutionary effort, the Bolivians were often willing to listen to and sometimes accept.

REESTABLISHMENT OF THE ARMY

What proved to be one of the fatal mistakes of the MNR government was its decision, a bit more than a year after it came to power, to reestablish the official armed forces. Although it sought to do this on a basis that would maintain the military in subordination to the civilian government, these efforts proved to be unsuccessful.

There were undoubtedly a number of reasons for the decision to reestablish the official army, navy, and air force. First, the government leaders discovered that young men, particularly Indians, used to being conscripted at the age of 18, continued to present themselves to the authorities for induction even after the dissolution of the military. The government leaders thought that it would be worthwhile to make use of this tradition, and to use the military conscripts for certain projects that were part of their economic development program. Second, it is probably the case that the government leaders in La Paz had a certain sense of insecurity with being dependent upon the goodwill of the militia, particularly the miners' militia, and felt the need for some counterforce to these civilians under arms. Finally, there was undoubtedly extensive pressure from the United States government for the reestablishment—and subsequently the strengthening—of the regular armed forces, and the MNR leaders undoubtedly felt that they would be more likely to get the economic aid they very much needed from the United States government if there were an established army, navy, and air force.

However, in reestablishing the official military, the MNR government sought to assure that it would always remain loyal to the civilian regime. Various approaches were taken to this end. On the one hand, those officers of the old military who were allowed to return to service were very carefully selected—or at least the MNR leaders thought they were. Preference was given to officers with whom the MNR had had close contact during their years in the political wilderness and for entry into the reestablished military academy to sons of MNR members or friends of the party. Furthermore, the MNR established its own "cells" in the various branches of the armed forces, and gave preference in terms of command and promotion to members of those cells. (Ironically, it was René Barrientos, head of the military cells of the MNR, who finally overthrew the MNR regime.)

Finally, the reorganized army was supposed to concentrate principally on economic projects, and its forces were concentrated in the eastern part of the country. At least during the first two MNR administrations, a point was made to keep only a small garrison in La Paz, where forces of the Carabineros and the workers' militia could presumably act as a counterweight to the army contingents.

Two of the major economic programs in which the military was involved were road building and colonization. The army engineers played a major role in constructing the highways in the highlands and in beginning the paving of the Cochabamba-Santa Cruz road.

However, more innovative was the work of the two colonization battalions organized by the new army. Young Indian recruits were placed in these units, which operated along the Cochabamba-Santa Cruz Highway, clearing land and preparing it for agriculture, and building rudimentary homes and other facilities. At the end of their military service, the enlisted men of the colonization battalions were offered land grants in the areas in which they had been operating, if they and their families would move there. Several thousand "graduates" of the colonization battalions accepted the offer and were a key element in developing the migratory stream from the valleys and Altiplano that started during the MNR regime.

During most of the MNR period, the military gave little evidence of overt political activity. However, as the government party tended to disintegrate, particularly during the second Paz Estenssoro administration, the political role of the military was strengthened. Furthermore, largely due to pressure from the U.S. government, the Bolivian military was more extensively and heavily armed than the MNR leaders had certainly originally intended it should be. The penultimate step toward the military again assuming an independent—and dominant— political role was undoubtedly the naming of General Barrientos, commander of the air force and head of the MNR military cells, as President Paz Estenssoro's running mate in the 1964 election.

POLITICAL CLIMATE OF THE MNR PERIOD

The twelve and one-half years of the regime of the MNR was the longest period of stable civilian government in Bolivia since the early 1900s. It was marked by three general elections and two peaceable transfers of the presidency from one man to another.

The MNR period was also one of relative political democracy, in Bolivian terms. Although the MNR was overwhelmingly the largest party and won every election without any difficulty, other parties did function and compete both for public attention and votes. The major opposition force during most of this period was the Falange Socialista Boliviana, which in fact, did not become a major party until the advent of the MNR to power, when it became the principal rallying point of those opposed to the revolution. To the Left of the MNR there were two more or less Stalinist parties—the Party of the Revolutionary Left (PIR), and the Communist Party—as well as the Trotskyists in the Partido Obrero Revolucionario (POR). These other leftist parties had some influence in the labor movement, and the Trotskyists may also have had some degree of peasant backing. However, they were no challenge for the MNR either in organized labor or in general politics.

A special word should be said about the POR. Some students of the Bolivian National Revolution have tended to exaggerate the influence and importance of this Trotskyist group in the revolutionary process. This has been due largely to a misunderstanding of the nature of the MNR leadership, particularly in the early years of the revolution.

During the first few months of the revolution, the Trotskyists seemed to have a great deal of influence, particularly in the newly established Central Obrera Boliviana. However, this influence was more apparent than real, as was amply demonstrated in October 1952.

The COB had an executive committee that met at least once a week to discuss union business and questions of high state policy. Ostensibly, the members of the executive committee were officials of the various unions and departmental labor federations that made up the COB. However, when such an official could not be present at an executive committee meeting, he was authorized to depute someone resident in La Paz to attend in his place.

As a result of this system, many of the POR members succeeded in getting themselves named as deputies for people in the provinces who could not attend weekly meetings in La Paz regularly. In those months, apparently, no great heed was paid to whether such a substitute delegate was a member of the MNR or the POR because until October no great divergences existed between the two parties. Furthermore, the hand of the POR was strengthened by the fact that many of the principal MNR labor leaders also held important posts in the revolutionary government. Hence, until and unless a serious controversy arose in the COB, Lechín (minister of mines), German Buitrón (minister of industry), and Ñuflo Chávez (minister of peasant affairs), and various other MNR labor leaders did not bother to attend the COB meetings.

Finally, the POR position was strengthened by the fact that José Zegada was the first general secretary of the COB. He had recently resigned from the POR, but still had a friendly disposition toward it. As second man in the organization, he ran its day-to-day affairs, since Executive Secretary Lechín did not have the time to do so. He also published the COB newspaper, which had a rather Trotskyist tone in its first months.

However, the fragility of the POR influence in the labor movement was revealed in October 1952 when a Trotskyist-dominated session of the COB executive went on record in opposition to the proposed decree nationalizing the "big three" tin mines because it provided for eventual compensation to the old owners. Thereupon, the MNR machine in the COB swung into action. A new meeting was called, attended this time by Lechín, Buitrón, Chávez, and a whole new list of substitute delegates, Movimientistas to a man, to replace the Trotskyists who until then had held these positions. This second meeting repudiated the motion of the earlier one and roundly endorsed the government's nationalization decree. From then on, the MNR labor leaders made it a point to be present at any important COB meeting, and the POR was reduced to one of several minority groups represented in the COB executive.

In those early months of the revolution when the POR seemed to be much more powerful than it actually was, there is no question about the fact that the principal Trotskyist leaders saw themselves playing Lenin to Paz Estenssoro's Kerensky, that is, they felt that they would sooner or later be able to capture the leadership of the revolution. However, they vastly overrated their own real influence and power, and many foreign observers of the revolution have, unfortunately, accepted this early Trotskyist version of what was transpiring in 1952. The mistakes in POR policy were recognized by 1954 by many of the party's trade union leaders, headed by Edwin Moller, and they withdrew from the POR to join the MNR, several (including Moller) running for Congress as MNR candidates in 1956.

It has been argued that Juan Lechín and other MNR labor leaders were at this time really more PORistas than Movimientistas. This is a serious misreading of the situation. During the first administration of Paz Estenssoro (1952-56) the MNR labor leaders were an integral and major part of the leadership of their party. When it, or the government, was attacked, they rallied to the support of the regime, from whatever quarter the attack came. It was not until the Siles administration that a serious breach occurred between the government and the left-wing MNR labor leaders, although even then it did not involve any split of the latter with the party.

Not only did various opposition political parties function during the dozen years of MNR rule, but this was also a period of relative respect for civil liberties. The late head of the Freedom of Press Committee of the Inter American Press Association, Jules Dubois, used to report regularly during these years that freedom of press did not exist in Bolivia. However, this was not in fact the case.

The complaint of Dubois and others was that two newspapers of the old regime, *La Razón* in La Paz and *Los Tiempos* in Cochabamba, had been seized at the onset of the revolution and had not been allowed to reopen. However, the fact was that there was a lively press during the MNR period and most of it was in the opposition. To replace *La Razón*, there was *El Diario*, which was basically a quite conservative paper and highly critical of the MNR government. In addition, a new paper, *Presencia*, of Catholic orientation appeared and it too was quite critical of the regime. Efforts by the MNR to establish its own daily to compete with these two failed. Finally, in addition to the daily press, most of the political groups active in the country had their weekly or monthly periodicals.

DISINTEGRATION OF THE MNR

The most fatal flaw in the MNR regime was the factionalism that developed during the Siles period (1956-60) and continued thereafter. Although during the first Paz Estenssoro government it had generally been recognized that there were several tendencies within the party, all were united behind the program of fundamental change that the MNR regime was carrying out. Certainly nothing at that time presaged any disintegration of the revolutionary party.

Indeed, during the first six years of the MNR regime, the party's influence in national politics seemed so overwhelming that it was the custom to suggest that there was being developed in Bolivia a system similar to that in Mexico where, although other parties function with more or less freedom, only one, the government party, ever wins important elections. However, by the end of the Siles period, the fissures in the MNR had become so serious that the Mexican model no longer was a viable one.

During the first Paz Estenssoro administration, there were generally recognized to be two major tendencies within the party. On the Left, led by Lechín and others among the trade union elements of the party, there were no basically different long-run objectives from those of the Right, or the party as a whole, but it was given perhaps to more revolutionary sounding rhetoric. It was certainly not Marxist-Leninist or anything approaching that.

The Right was generally conceded to be led by Hernán Siles. However, it was not clear exactly what being on the Right meant insofar as the objectives and practical policies of the regime were concerned. In neither faction, and seeking to mediate between them, was Paz Estenssoro.

When it came time to choose a successor to Paz Estenssoro, the party agreed to name Siles from the Right for president, and Chávez from the Left for vice-president. They were duly elected and took office in August 1956. However, early in the Siles administration there came the crisis over the stabilization program, as a consequence of which Chávez resigned the vice-presidency, and Lechín tried to organize a general strike in the mines against the government's policies. With the passing of this crisis, peace seemed to have been restored to the MNR ranks, and President Siles very clearly did not support an attempt by some of his labor union sympathizers to organize a rival to the COB controlled by Lechín.

The next crisis in the MNR came in connection with the choice of a candidate for the 1960 presidential election. Walter Guevara Arze, foreign minister and associated with the Siles wing, certainly felt that he had been promised by the other top leaders of the party that he would be the MNR nominee. However, Paz Estenssoro decided that he would return from his post as ambassador to Great Britain and run for a second time. Virtually all of the other leaders of the party accepted this, particularly after he agreed to have Lechín as his vice-presidential nominee, with the promise that Lechín would be the 1964 MNR candidate. Walter Guevara Arze, however, did not accept it, and withdrew from the party to form his own Partido Revolucionario Auténtico (Authentic Revolutionary Party—PRA), and to make a hopeless run against Paz Estenssoro in the election.

Guevara Arze became a bitter critic of the MNR and of the second Paz Estenssoro administration. However, he did not take any substantial portion of the party leadership and rank and file with him when he left the party. Much more serious—and well-nigh fatal—was the split of Lechín with the MNR.

There is little question about the fact that Lechín had been promised by the other MNR leaders the party's nomination in 1964. However, there was considerable opposition to his nomination within the party. Perhaps more important, it is reported that the United States embassy was strongly against the candidacy of Lechín, and at least implied that the substantial economic help that was being extended to the MNR government by the United States would dry up should Lechín ever assume the presidency.

Whatever the reasons for their decision, the majority of the leaders of the MNR finally concluded that they could not give the party's nomination to Lechín in the 1964 election. In the face of that situation, the only leader strong enough to defeat Lechin was Paz Estenssoro, and he became candidate for re-election for a third term.

There are those who argue that Paz Estenssoro had been planning for his second reelection for several years. It is true that in 1962 the constitution was altered to permit an incumbent president to run for immediate reelection, something which had until then been forbidden. However, this move was made without any notable opposition from other elements of the MNR leadership.

Denied the MNR presidential nomination, Lechín withdrew from the Movimiento Nacionalista Revolucionario with his labor followers, and organized the Revolutionary Party of the Nationalist Left (Partido Revolucionario de la Izquierda Nacionalista—PRIN). His new party named him to run against Paz Estenssoro in the 1964 election, but withdrew his candidacy before the voting on the grounds that the elections had been rigged by the government.

Meanwhile, the MNR had renominated Paz Estenssoro. However, there was some confusion this time concerning his running mate. After first naming a civilian, the party leadership suddenly changed its mind as the result of open pressure from its own military cell and replaced him with General René Barrientos as candidate for vice-president.

During the process of the election campaign, there were further defections from the MNR. The most notable of these was ex-President Siles, who finally expressed his opposition to Paz Estenssoro's candidacy, and urged him to withdraw. With the exit of Siles, Paz Estenssoro remained as the only major figure among those who had led the Bolivian National Revolution a dozen years before to still be in the MNR.

Paz Estenssoro won the election with little opposition. However, instead of being the beginning of another four-year term, the reelection signaled the beginning of the end of the revolutionary regime.

OVERTHROW OF THE REVOLUTIONARY REGIME

Plotting against the Paz Estenssoro government had begun even before the president had been reelected. In all probability, the plotters included not only the principal leaders of the armed forces, but also Siles, Lechín, and many other former leaders of the revolutionary government.

The leaders of the armed forces hesitated to move against the government. They were afraid that to do so would provoke a civil war since they knew that the peasantry in the great majority remained loyal to the MNR as a party and to Paz Estenssoro as the man who had signed the agrarian reform decree that had given them their land. The military leaders feared they would have to fight against an aroused and perhaps enraged peasant militia if they made any move to overthrow the president.

An incident only ten days before the soldiers moved convinced them they could do so with impunity. Late in October the government was faced not only with demonstrations and seizure of some of the mines by the miners, but also with a student strike and demonstrations in La Paz. To deal with these situations, President Paz Estenssoro conferred with the army commander-in-chief, General Alfredo Ovando. They compared notes on the relative strength of the regular army forces and the peasant militia. Elements of both forces were used, but the fact was the Paz Estensssoro had been forced to disclose to one of the conspirators against him (which he did not know, of course) how weak and poorly armed the peasant militia really were.

Sometime before this, the government had placed orders in Argentina for substantial quantities of new small arms for the peasant militia, but the Argentine military had refused to permit their delivery to Bolivia. As a consequence, the peasant militia were equipped mainly with what had been taken from the Bolivian army in 1952 and in large part consisted of weapons of Chaco War vintage, whereas the regular armed forces had recently been extensively re-equipped with more or less up-to-date U.S. armament.

Thus assured that they would face little resistance from the peasant militia, the military leaders completed their plans for overthrowing the Paz Estenssoro government. They chose a particularly propitious day for their coup—November 4. The weekend before that had been the Day of the Dead, which is widely celebrated by the Bolivian Indians by first taking flowers to the cemeteries for the graves of deceased relatives and then by becoming exceedingly intoxicated. The upshot of this situation was that when the coup began, and Paz Estenssoro sent 50 trucks to nearby Indian communities to mobilize peasant militiamen, only 1 of the 50 vehicles returned with armed peasants. Thus the effective opposition of the peasants to the ouster of the government was virtually nonexistent.

Faced with the coup, Paz Estenssoro was sure that its leader was General Barrientos. On the other hand, he thought that he could count on the loyalty of General Ovando, with whom on several occasions he had conferred with regard to his doubts about Barrientos' loyalty. However, when President Paz Estenssoro called in General Ovando and asked him to move against the rebellious soldiers, Ovando professed to be unable to control them—whereas, in fact, he was one of the leaders of the move to oust the government. The comedy was fully played out when General Ovando finally accompanied now ex-President Paz Estenssoro to the airport to begin his trip into exile.

CONCLUSION

Thus came to an inglorious end the 12 years of government of the Movimiento Nacionalista Revolucionario. These had been years that had brought truly revolutionary transformation of Bolivian society, and had even profoundly altered the basis of national politics. However, through internal weaknesses and policy errors, the MNR failed to establish a firm basis for democratic civilian government. Although continuing to enjoy the support of the great majority of the people of Bolivia, the MNR (now split in various fragments) was not again able to win power. Its overthrow began a long period of political musical chairs in which one ambitious military leader succeeded another in the presidential palace, the Palacio Quemado.

7

POSTREVOLUTIONARY BOLIVIA

Since November 1964, Bolivia has had more than a dozen presidents. Only three of these have been civilians. Only one took office as the result of general elections, and in that case the validity of the poll can be seriously questioned. Although many of the accomplishments of the revolution remained, the country clearly slid into a kind of militarism that was worse than anything it had experienced before in the twentieth century.

AFTER THE OUSTER OF PAZ ESTENSSORO

With the overthrow of President Paz Estenssoro and the government of the MNR, there was a short political honeymoon. Ex-President Hernán Siles, ex-Foreign Minister Walter Guevara Arze, and ex-Vice-President Juan Lechín were among the one-time leaders of the Bolivian National Revolution who greeted with enthusiasm its demise. Needless to say, the surviving political figures of the old regime also were ecstatic about the ouster of the MNR.

On the other hand, ex-President Paz Estenssoro and those who had been associated with him in the final phases of the revolutionary regime were exiled or jailed for longer or shorter periods of time. Their faction of the MNR was suppressed, at least for the time being, although other political groups continued to function more or less normally.

There was apparently some confusion concerning just who would rule once Paz Estenssoro had been ousted. General Barrientos first became head of a new military junta. On November 6, it was announced that he and General

Ovando would serve as co-presidents, but Ovando resigned the post within 24 hours, leaving Barrientos as the single head of the regime. In May 1965 General Ovando again became co-president with Barrientos, and in January 1966 when Barrientos resigned to run for president in approaching elections, Ovando was left as the single president of the provisional regime.

The political honeymoon did not last for very long. The first major cause of conflict between the new government and civilians who had supported its seizure of power came over the policies to be followed in the mining industry. The military leaders remained committed to the Triangular Plan for rationalization of the tin-mining industry that had been launched by the Paz Estenssoro government several years before. This commitment soon brought them into conflict with Lechín and the miners' federation.

Finally, in June 1965 there was a showdown between the miners and the military government when it dismissed large numbers of "excess" miners and enacted a general reduction in the miners' wages. The mine workers went out on general strike. The government, determined to break the miners' resistance, ordered the army to occupy the mining camps. There was considerable fighting between miners and soldiers, and the casualties among the miners were numerous. This battle (known as the St. John's Day massacre) has gone down in the annals of the miners' federation as one of their most bitter and bloody defeats.

THE BARRIENTOS REGIME

Once they felt themselves securely enough in power, the military men called general elections for June 1966. The government's candidate was obviously General Barrientos. He organized a political party to support his aspirations to be constitutional chief executive, the Popular Christian Movement (Movimiento Popular Cristiano—MPC). Barrientos chose as his vice-presidential running mate a civilian, Luis Adolfo Siles Salinas, the half-brother of ex-President Siles and head of the small Social Democratic Party that had been a vocal but not very important opposition group during the MNR regime.

Once the process of registering parties for the election began, the question arose whether the MNR should be allowed to participate. The government decided it should, but refused to recognize either of the principal currents of the party, those of ex-Presidents Paz Estenssoro and Siles, as the "official" MNR. Instead, the regime's electoral authorities gave official status to a splinter movement headed by Victor Andrade, who had been Bolivian ambassador to the United States throughout most of the MNR period. Several other "opposition" parties were recognized, although it was a foregone conclusion that General Barrientos would be the victor.

Aside from the fact that he had been chosen in what was far from a democratic election, Barrientos was a comparatively good president. He spoke

Quechua, and was strongly committed at least to the agrarian reform aspect of the revolution. He was the one president who seemed to understand the need for giving the Indian peasants technical aid, advice, credit, and other help to integrate their peasant subsistence economy into the wider economy of the nation. With the cooperation of the United States foreign aid program, he launched a number of programs for the Indians, including the establishment of sheep dips to aid in fleecing sheep, helping to upgrade wheat, potato, and corn crops, and aid in marketing some of their products. He also gave considerable impetus to the spread of schools in the rural areas.

There is little doubt that Barrientos enjoyed considerable popularity among the Indians. His ability to speak one of their languages undoubtedly helped in this regard. Also, he was in frequent touch with local peasant groups, traveling constantly around the countryside, getting to know various communities and their leaders, accepting their hospitality, and inspecting the various activities his government was trying to do for the Indians.

The support of the peasants for the Barrientos regime was of great importance in 1967 when Ché Guevara attempted to organize a guerrilla campaign in Bolivia. There were many errors of judgment involved in Ché's campaign—for instance, the large number of Cubans speaking a strange Spanish to the Bolivians, the particular area in which Guevara chose to establish himself, and his failure to gain the support of any significant Bolivian far-Left group. However, the greatest mistake of all proved to be Ché's hope that he would be able to mobilize the Bolivian peasants against the regime of General Barrientos. As Ché complained in his diary, the response of the Indians the guerrillas encountered was in no way friendly, and more often than not they informed the Bolivian authorities of where the guerrillas were and what they were doing.

Although enjoying considerable backing among the peasants, President Barrientos was highly unpopular with the urban workers, and particularly with the miners. His government severely restricted the rights of the unions, not allowing them to have free elections of their officials. Troops continued from time to time to occupy the mining camps. Large numbers of workers who had been dismissed during the provisional regime of 1964-66 because they were deemed "in excess" in the mines or because of their trade union or political activities remained without jobs.

It was on one of his trips around the countryside on April 27, 1969, that Barrientos was killed in an accident when the helicopter in which he was taking off from a meeting ran into an electric wire. Subsequently, it was for long a matter of debate whether Barrientos' helicopter had been shot before it ran into the wire, although most people accepted the version that it was the pilot's error in not avoiding entanglement which caused the accident fatal to both the pilot and the president.

THE OVANDO GOVERNMENT

President Barrientos was succeeded immediately by his vice-president, Luis Adolfo Siles Salinas. The new chief executive promised to continue the policies of his predecessor, and did so in most regards. He somewhat relaxed controls over the labor movement, but was not in office long enough to develop fully a new labor policy.

With Barrientos' death, the real power in Bolivia was in the hands of General Alfredo Ovando, and on September 26, 1969, he removed President Siles Salinas, and took over the presidential office himself. The ascension of General Ovando once more to the presidency was generally interpreted as a move to the Left in Bolivian politics. He brought into his first cabinet a number of young men of the Left not associated with any of the existing major parties, most notably Marcelo Quiroga Santa Cruz and Alberto Bailey.

Ovando proclaimed his to be a "revolutionary nationalist" government dedicated to the ideals of the 1952 revolution, but wanted to do away with the alleged "perversion" of these ideals by the MNR and President Barrientos. He appealed to the labor movement, in particular, for its support.

As a practical matter, President Ovando repealed the decree-law of Barrientos that had required government approval of all elected union officials. As a result, the labor movement reorganized. The Central Obrera Boliviana was openly reestablished, with Lechín again as its principal leader. The Ovando government replaced in their jobs many miners who had been dismissed since 1964. Various national unions held new congresses.

The Federación Sindical de Trabajadores Mineros held its congress in April 1970 in Catavi. At this session Lechín was reelected executive secretary of the miners' federation, and a list of candidates for other offices that he favored was chosen over a rival slate of some Communists and Trotskyites in the federation. The still substantial following of the MNR among the miners supported Lechín against his far-Left rivals in this congress.

One of the first acts of the Ovando government was to expropriate the concession of the Gulf Oil Company in the Santa Cruz region. It was then the only foreign oil enterprise operating in the country, having received its concession during the government of Hernán Siles. Although the labor movement and elements of the political Left supported the expropriation with enthusiasm, they were highly critical of the Ovando government's promise to compensate the Gulf Company.

General Ovando's efforts to build a wide basis of support were only partly successful. In spite of his policies in 1969–70, trade unionists remembered that he had been in charge of the troops that had invaded the mining camps in June 1965. The orthodox MNR around ex-President Paz Estenssoro would not forgive Ovando the part he had played in the overthrow of the MNR regime. Ovando did not have the same concern as Barrientos for the welfare and progress of the peasants, and his attempts to keep in existence the "peasant-military alliance" that Barrientos had boasted of and to some degree had enjoyed, were not particularly successful.

Finally, General Ovando faced considerable opposition from those within the military who had helped him to power in the first place. There were right-wing officers who were highly suspicious of his overtures to the labor movement, particularly the miners, and other military leaders who were shocked by the scandals, including assassinations of some political leaders and a well-known newspaper editor, scandals with which Ovando was rumored to be connected.

President Ovando was thus under very strong political pressures from various quarters. In May 1979 he gave in to pressures from the Right by dismissing from his cabinet most of the young radicals whom he had brought in when he seized the presidency. However, this move probably only postponed his overthrow, and certainly did not prevent it.

THE TORRES GOVERNMENT

On October 6, 1970, the armed forces moved to oust President Ovando. However, there resulted a couple days of profound confusion. A military junta, consisting of Efraín Guachalla, Fernando Sattori, and Admiral Alberto Albarracín took over, and seemed ready to install General Rogelio Miranda as the new president. However, this group represented a far-Right element within the army and national politics, and it immediately aroused strong opposition, not only within the armed forces but in the streets of La Paz and in the mining camps.

The upshot of this situation was that the junta lasted only a little more than 24 hours. General Juan José Torres came into office with the support not only of decisive elements of the armed forces, but also of the Central Obrera Boliviana, the miners' federation, and various other civilian elements, particularly those of the Left. However, General Torres was forced to keep in their posts many of the military men, including army commander Luis Reque Terán, who had at first supported the junta.

In any case, General Torres was a peculiar person to become the symbol of the Left in Bolivian politics. He had been the officer commanding the troops that fought and finally rounded up and killed the guerrilla force led by Ché Guevara. It has been suggested that it was exactly because of this that General Torres cooperated so extensively with the far Left during his short period in power, seeking by that policy to live down his previous reputation.

The 11 months of the Torres regime were characterized by considerable chaos. In some cases, the workers unions took over control of the mines. Some private agricultural enterprises were seized by "revolutionaries." Certain businesses in La Paz and other cities were forced to pay substantial amounts to groups that were threatening nationalization.

Many of the elements of the Left, particularly some of the Trotskyites, felt that the situation could be taken advantage of to bring about the quick establishment of a "socialist" government, something President Torres himself promised as a long-range goal of his regime.

One of the factors that seemed to characterize the months of the Torres regime as a "prerevolutionary" period was the establishment of the so-called Popular Assembly (Asamblea Popular). This was a species of soviet (probably modeled on those of 1917 Russia) consisting of delegates from workers' unions, peasant groups, and various political parties. According to the rules established by those who had organized the Popular Assembly, 60 percent of its members came from working-class groups, with the miners holding a large share, 30 percent represented salaried workers and peasants, and 10 percent directly represented the various political parties that participated in the Asamblea Popular. Most notable was the small representation of peasant groups in spite of the fact that the peasants still made up the considerable majority of the population.

Various political groups were represented among the members of the Popular Assembly. These included the factions of the Trotskyist POR led by Hugo González Moscoso and Guillermo Lora. Lora himself played a major role in the deliberations of the Asamblea. Both the pro-Moscow and pro-Peking Communist parties were represented as were the PRIN of Lechín, the left-wing element of the Christian Democrats, and two new parties, the Movimiento de Izquierda Revolucionaria (MIR—the Movement of the Revolutionary Left), also of Christian Democratic origin, and the Partido Socialista led by Marcelo Quiroga Santa Cruz, which had broken off from the MNR. Most surprising in view of its critical attitude toward General Torres was that the MNR temporarily reunited under the joint exile leadership of Paz Estenssoro and Siles had the largest single political group in the Asamblea.

The Popular Assembly held its first session in the Congress building in La Paz on May 1, 1971, after a May Day demonstration and parade in which President Torres himself participated. The only business of the day was the election of officers, with Lechín chosen president of the Asamblea Popular.

The body met again on June 24 for a plenary session. The meeting passed (successfully) a resolution demanding the removal of the U.S. Peace Corps from Bolivia and others for workers' control of the mining industry, nationalization of the "middle" and "small" private mining firms, and various other measures. It also urged the arming of the people and pledged that in case of any right-wing attempt to oust the Torres government, the Asamblea Popular would organize and lead the armed resistance.

The Popular Assembly had no formal legislative power. President Torres made it clear that he did not regard it as the national congress. The regime did not last long enough for the relationship between the government and the

Popular Assembly to be clarified. The Asamblea Popular remained a pressure group, exerting the influence of the labor movement and the political parties on the Torres regime, which as a de facto government continued to legislate by decree.

The only important piece of legislation enacted by the Torres regime was a decree expropriating the Matilde mine, the largest still in private hands. It had belonged to a U.S. firm.

THE NATIONALIST POPULAR FRONT

On August 21-22, 1971, the government of President Torres was over-thrown. Its fall came at the hands of elements of the armed forces, supported by the civilian Nationalist Popular Front (Frente Popular Nacionalista—FPN), an unlikely alliance of the MNR and the Falange Socialista Boliviana. This coup installed as president Colonel Hugo Banzer, who was to prove the most durable of the military dictators holding office subsequent to the fall of the MNR in 1964.

Colonel Banzer had been opposed to the Torres regime from the start. As commander of the military academy, he had organized an abortive coup as early as January 1971. When it failed, he had fled abroad. Outside the country, he clearly entered into contact not only with the country's two largest political parties, but also with foreign governments, most notably the military regime in Brazil, which gave him substantial help in his efforts to overthrow the Torres government.

The insurrection led by Banzer began in the eastern provincial capital of Santa Cruz. Once the rebels had established control there, they began to receive pledges of support from military units in virtually all other provincial cities. Finally, late on August 21, most of the garrison of La Paz also went over to the insurrection. In most provincial cities, the union and party leaders who had been pledging to fight "to the death" against any attempt to oust Torres were no-where to be found; in La Paz, where there was some working-class and student resistance, it was disorganized and certainly not directed by the national political and labor leaders.

The new regime was, from a political point of view, a very peculiar one. It was pictured by its leaders as an alliance of the armed forces with the MNR and the Falange Socialista Boliviana. Paz Estenssoro and other exiled MNR leaders returned to Bolivia, and during the first months of the Banzer government, Paz Estenssoro was undoubtedly one of the principal political and economic advisers of the president.

The two parties, which until August 1971 had been mortal enemies, pro-ceeded to divide most posts (except those which the military retained for them-selves) among their members. Falange leader Mario Gutiérrez became foreign minister; and although Paz Estenssoro did not himself take a post in the government, he nominated a number of young MNR leaders for cabinet and sub-cabinet positions, principally those dealing with economic problems. Even such posts as those of university rectors were divided between the MNR and the Falange.

Although the MNR and the Falange were officially partners in the first stage of the Banzer government, their freedom of action—particularly that of the MNR—was severely limited. Thus, the MNR, with its principal backing in the countryside, was specifically forbidden by its military partners to try to re-organize the party structure among the Indians. It was free to reestablish its organizations in the cities, but the countryside was off-limits to organizers of the party.

This anomalous situation had one important long-range political effect. It brought about splits in both of the parties that participated in the Nationalist Popular Front. In the case of the MNR, it brought about a definitive break between Paz Estenssoro and Hernán Siles, with the latter opposing participation in the Banzer government and withdrawing his supporters from the MNR to establish the so-called Movimiento Nacionalista Revolucionario de Izquierda (Nationalist Revolutionary Movement of the Left—MNRI). Subsequently, when Paz Estenssoro broke with the Banzer government, some of his followers decided to continue in it and they organized their own version—of short duration—of the MNR. The Falange also suffered a major schism, the first in its history, when Carlos Valverde, the party's principal figure in the Santa Cruz region, broke with the majority of the party, which remained under the leadership of Mario Gutiérrez.

During the period of the Nationalist Popular Front, the regime was com-mitted to holding new general elections in due time. Decisions to this end were taken by the regime. It was decided to use the electoral law under which Presi-dent Barrientos had won in 1966. President Banzer decided that he would be a candidate in the forthcoming election and was promptly endorsed by the Nationalist Popular Front, that is, the Paz Estenssoro wing of the MNR and the Falange.

The situation in the labor movement was a confusing one during the period of the FPN government. The prepotential power that organized labor seemed to have during the Torres government totally collapsed. Most of the leading trade unionists fled the country with the ouster of President Torres. Although the government did not during this period take any overt steps against the labor movement and there were elections within at least some of the unions to fill the posts of those who had fled, the Nationalist Popular Front regime did little to win over the workers to the new regime. There were several strikes, particularly in La Paz, and the government did not show a particularly favorable attitude toward the workers in these incidents.

During the less than two and a half years during which the Nationalist Popu-lar Front existed in actuality—it officially continued for some time after it had ceased to have any reality—little effort was made to renew the revolution that the MNR had begun in 1952. The MNR ministers in the government were principally concerned with such economic questions as limiting inflation and improving the country's balance of payments position. Ex-President Paz Estenssoro himself professed to see these economic questions as the most important immediate ones.

It was disagreement over economic issues that finally brought an effective end to the Nationalist Popular Front regime. Late in 1973 President Banzer agreed to a sizable devaluation of the Bolivian monetary unit. This move was strongly opposed by Paz Estenssoro, and several MNR officials resigned over the issue. The ex-president made little secret concerning his position, to the point that he became a serious embarrassment to the Banzer government. As a result, early in January 1974 Paz Estenssoro was arrested and sent once again into exile. That action effectively put an end to the regime of the Nationalist Popular Front, although it continued to use that name for some months thereafter.

THE UNIPERSONAL REGIME OF HUGO BANZER

After the deportation of Paz Estenssoro, it was quite clear that the government in power was completely under the control of President Banzer. It was only a few months until all pretense of party participation in the regime was ended, and from then on all ministers and other top officials served only at the command of the president.

The basis of support in the Banzer regime during its last four and a half years in power was clearly the military. During most of this period, the cabinet was overwhelmingly composed of armed forces officers, the only civilians usually being nonpolitical technicians. It was Banzer's continuing ability to control the army that assured his remarkably long tenure in office.

The regime met widespread civilian opposition. Although a pretense was maintained that there existed a "military peasant alliance," and individual peasant caciques were always available to maintain this fiction, the Banzer government's relations with the peasantry were in fact very troubled. The most serious conflict between the regime and the peasants took place in the Cochabamba region late in January 1974. A substantial group of peasants, angered by extensive price increases (which the government had just enacted) for items they had to buy, blockaded the Cochabamba-Santa Cruz Highway, refusing to allow trucks or other vehicles to travel along this key road. After declaring a "state of siege" in the Cochabamba area, Banzer sent in army units, and they shot their way through the blockade, killing and wounding many peasants in the process.

After this incident, the military peasant alliance was fiction. However, Banzer was careful not to challenge the right of the peasants to continue to hold the land that they had received in the agrarian reform of the revolutionary government of the 1950s. Therefore, for the most part, the peasants, as was their traditional wont, contented themselves with going about their own business and not directly challenging the regime.

The Banzer government had more difficulties with the organized workers. Strikes continued to plague the regime. Although they did not critically endanger the government, General Banzer and his associates decided that the root of their trouble with the labor movement was that it was "political." Logically, then, the government decided that it would "depoliticize" organized labor.

To this end, a Law of Compulsory Civil Service, supposedly analagous to the military conscription statute, was enacted in November 1974. It provided that the president could "draft" people to take a job in the government or to head a union or professional association. Refusal could result in jail for two years.

In conformity with this law, on November 9, 1974, the government declared all trade union leadership posts vacant. It then proceeded under the Compulsory Civil Service system to appoint most of the elected union officials on each level of the union hierarchy as "coordinators" of their respective organizations. In the great majority of cases, the trade unionists involved accepted the new state of affairs, and continued to function as government coordinators rather than elected officials.

The only area in which this procedure met widespread resistance was the mines. There, virtually all of the union leaders refused to accept the posts of coordinator, and as a result they were jailed. However, as a consequence of strikes and demonstrations, the government decided to back down and freed most of the union leaders, who resumed their old positions. The government, in a face-saving gesture, "appointed" them to those posts, although being careful not to call the mine union officials coordinators.

The somewhat tenuous logic of the government in establishing the Law of Compulsory Civil Service and applying it to the labor movement was that the coordinators as government appointees would no longer be "political." Furthermore, the Minister of Labor, Lieutenant Colonel Mario Vargas, and others involved in this exercise hoped that after four or five years of such "apolitical" leadership, the old unionists, owing loyalty to one or another political party, would have passed from the scene, to be succeeded by new labor leaders without political connections. The government proposed to propound a new labor code that would further assure the "nonpolitical" leadership of the organized labor movement, something it did not get around to doing before the Banzer regime passed from the scene.

In seeking to develop civilian support, President Banzer actively reopened the issue of Bolivia's obtaining an outlet to the Pacific Ocean, which it had not had since the War of the Pacific almost a century before. This effort included renewal of diplomatic relations with Chile, which had been cut off several years before, and proposals by the Bolivian government that the treaty of 1904 be reopened and Chile concede Bolivia a Pacific port. The Chilean government of

General Augusto Pinochet finally replied to the suggestions of the Banzer regime by offering Bolivia a strip of territory north of the city of Arica. On the ocean this territory would be eight miles wide, further inland it would be broader. Chile, Pinochet claimed, would be willing to help Bolivia build a new port on the ocean.

There were several difficulties with this proposal that proved insurmountable, as President Pinochet undoubtedly knew they would. First, the territory that Chile proposed to cede had been taken from Peru, not Bolivia, in the 1879 war, and according to the Chilean-Peruvian treaty of 1929 could only be transferred to a third power with Peru's consent. The Peruvian government promptly made it clear that such consent would never be forthcoming. In addition, Pinochet's proposal provided for Bolivia to give Chile certain territories in the interior in exchange for the land it would cede to Bolivia. Such a proposal—particularly since the land involved was rumored to contain extensive minerals—was not acceptable to anyone in Bolivia.

By the time President Banzer left office, the whole charade over the "exit to the Sea" had collapsed.

One of the reasons explaining the comparatively long tenure in office of the Banzer regime was the relative prosperity the country enjoyed during much of the period. The oil industry expanded modestly and provided foreign exchange in addition to that of tin mining, a factor aided by the world oil crisis. Devaluation of the Bolivian currency helped to provide protection to domestic manufacturing industries. Finally, the program of development of the east, which had been begun under the revolutionary government in the 1950s and early 1960s, began to pay substantial dividends during the Banzer years. Considerable growth and diversification of agriculture in the Oriente took place, and there were also some agricultural and oil-based manufacturing firms that developed there during those years.

LAST MONTHS OF THE BANZER REGIME

The event that finally sealed the doom of the seemingly impervious regime of General Banzer was the necessity, experienced by many Latin American dictatorships, to somehow make itself "constitutional." The only way to achieve this was to go through at least the motions of an election.

Once the Nationalist Popular Front ceased effectively to exist, the idea of an election was postponed more or less indefinitely. After first promising to hold an election in 1975 and then canceling those plans, the government kept postponing the issue. However, by the later months of 1977, it again became a rather pressing issue.

President Banzer promised that elections would be held in 1978. However, for many months it was not clear whether this would be merely an exercise for the purpose of transforming a de facto president to a "constitutional" one, or whether there would be a real test at the ballot box. All indications until early in 1978 indicated that the former was more likely.

The event that completely changed the Bolivian political picture was a "hunger strike" in early January 1978 organized by citizens without noted political connections, but with the backing of the hierarchy of the Catholic Church. The strikers, who occupied the cathedral and other churches as well as the building of the Catholic daily *Presencia*, demanded complete amnesty for all political prisoners and exiles. Although police and troops were first used to attack some of the hunger strikers, the church reacted vigorously. Archbishop Jorge Manrique delivered a sermon in the presence of President Banzer in which he denounced the "lack of human feeling" of the government, and threatened to decree a three-day interdict if the government did not give in to the hunger strikers.

The upshot of this situation was a complete surrender on the part of the Banzer government. The Minister of Interior signed an official agreement with the hunger strikers conceding all of their demands. This action demonstrated the grave weakness of the regime.

The first to respond to this evidence of weakness was the labor movement. The underground leadership of the Central Obrera Boliviana called upon the members of the unions no longer to recognize the "coordinators." The unions of telephone workers, railroaders, and others announced that they would immediately hold new elections for their officials. Nine elected officials of the miners' federation came out of hiding and occupied the headquarters of their federation in La Paz without interference on the part of the government.

With these events, the defenses of the government were thoroughly breached. Exiles streamed back, political prisoners were released, and the political parties reorganized. The labor movement also reorganized and the Central Obrera Boliviana held yet another convention, where once again Lechín was chosen as its principal official.

THE 1978 ELECTION

With the loosening of the Banzer dictatorship as a result of the events of January 1978, attention centered on the election scheduled for late June. The official candidate, having the supposed blessings of President Banzer, was General Juan Pereda Asbún of the air force. The only recognized political force supporting him, aside from the government, was a motley group of "Barrientistas"—military men and civilians who had been particularly closely associated with the late President Barrientos.

One of the principal strengths of the government candidate proved to be the multiplicity of nominees running against him. The most important of these were ex-President Hernán Siles, who was backed by a coalition the most important elements of which were his MNRI and the party of young ex-Christian Democrats, the MIR; and ex-President Paz Estenssoro, who ran as the candidate of his own MNR faction, which in this election took the name Historic Nationalist Revolutionary Movement (Movimiento Nacionalista Revolucionario-Historico—MNRH). Walter Guevara Arze of the first dissident group to break from the MNR in 1960, was Paz Estenssoro's vice-presidential nominee. The eight other candidates included men backed by the Christian Democratic Party, the PRIN of Lechín, the Socialist Party of Marcelo Quiroga Santa Cruz (former minister in the Ovando government), and various others.

When the votes were finally cast, they were counted to show that the government nominee. General Pereda Asbún, had won. However, the opposition immediately raised the cry that Pereda Asbún's victory had been achieved by fraud, a charge corroborated by the fact that the number said to have voted exceeded by 50,000 the number of registered voters. Even General Pereda Asbún finally conceded that the election had been fraudulent, and asked that the results be canceled, which the electoral court then proceeded to do.

However, this did not end the story of the 1978 election. General Pereda Asbún flew to Santa Cruz, where he led a rebellion of the local garrison, which was soon joined by that of Cochabamba. The rebels demanded the resignation of President Banzer, and the installation of General Pereda Asbún on the grounds that he had "won" the election. Without support even from the garrison in La Paz, President Banzer resigned, and General Asbún became the new president of Bolivia.

THE 1979 ELECTION

President Pereda Asbún's tenure in office was a stormy and short one. Soon after assuming office, he pictured his regime as a transitional one, paving the way for new elections. However, he announced postponement of those new elections until sometime in 1980. None of the civilian political groupings was willing to accept such a long period.

The opposition to Pereda Asbún came not only from the civilians, but from within the army and from ex-President Banzer, who had been Pereda Asbún's sponsor. As a result, the president was kept constantly busy mending his fences within the armed forces, and was forced to make what he and some observers considered humiliating concessions in several labor disputes that took place during his short period in office.

Finally, at the end of November 1978, President Pereda Asbún was overthrown by yet another military coup, headed by the army commander, General David Padilla. The Padilla government immediately stated that its task was solely that of preparing for and presiding over new elections, and he set the date of July 1, 1979, for these.

In preparation for the new elections there was some realignment of forces. The Christian Democratic Party and the pro-Peking Communist Party joined the group behind ex-President Paz Estenssoro, with a Christian Democrat supplanting Walter Guevara Arze (who chose to run for the Senate) as Paz Estenssoro's running mate. Ex-President Siles chose a young leader of the MIR, Jaime Paz (a nephew of Paz Estenssoro) as his vice-presidential candidate. A new entry this time was ex-President Banzer, who had organized his own party, Nationalist Democratic Action (Acción Democrática Nacionalista—ADN).

In the July 1, 1979 election, Siles was the leader, with Paz Estenssoro fairly close behind him, and General Banzer as a poor third. None of the candidates had a majority of the votes, and as a result, the final choice of a new president was thrown into Congress. There, in spite of extended efforts to reach an agreement between the Siles and Paz Estenssoro forces, the best that they could agree to was to elect an interim president to serve until still a third round of elections could be held in 1980.

The choice for interim president fell on Walter Guevara Arze. He had been chosen as president of the Senate, and thus was constitutionally in line if no agreement on electing a constitutional president and vice-president could be reached. Guevara Arze had aspired to the presidency a far back as 1960 when, upon being denied the nomination of the MNR, he had broken away to form his own small party, the Authentic Revolutionary Party (PRA). Guevara Arze took office on August 6, 1979, the normal date for a newly elected president to take over.

THE 1980 ELECTION AND AFTERMATH

President Walter Guevara Arze scheduled the third round of elections for May 1980. However, a great deal was to happen before those elections could be held. Although Guevara Arze enjoyed the support or at least tolerance of the major contending groups in Congress, his acceptance by the military was only provisional at best. Ex-President David Padilla, whom Guevara Arze named as head of the armed forces, had great difficulty in keeping his uniformed comrades in line behind the Guevara Arze government.

One serious problem was the insistence of Congress to investigate various crimes, including several murders, that had occurred during the Banzer regime. Although General Padilla and other officers insisted that Banzer's government had not been a regime "of the armed forces," and therefore the investigation represented no threat to the armed forces as an institution, many of his fellow generals and colonels remained unconvinced. The major mover of the investigation was deputy Marcelo Quiroga Santa Cruz of the small Socialist Party.

Discontent in the military finally spilled over on November 1, when a new coup, this time led by Colonel Alberto Natusch Busch, overthrew President

Guevara Arze. However, the deposed president refused to accept his ouster, and the Congress, first meeting openly and then forced to gather in secret, supported Guevara Arze. Meanwhile, a general strike against the military coup swept the country and was effective both in the mines and in the country's major cities.

The upshot of this situation was that both Walter Guevara Arze and Colonel Natusch Busch withdrew from the presidency. Congress thereupon elected a new president, the first woman to hold this post, Lidia Gueiler. She had been associated with Lechín's PRIN, but had broken with it in 1979 to support the presidential candidacy of Paz Estenssoro. Many years before she had been a Trotskyist, and had been among those who left the POR in 1954 to join the MNR.

With the denouement of the November 1979 crisis, preparations for the 1980 election went forward. Again, the two major nominees were Siles and Paz Estenssoro, and the third nominee was ex-President Banzer. The alignments behind these candidates that had prevailed in 1979 were not substantially altered in the 1980 contest.

One event that occurred only about a month before the new election had great importance for the future. This was the appointment of General Luis García Meza as commander of the army early in 1980. He had held this same post during the two-week regime of President Natusch Busch in November 1979, and had been forced to give it up when Natusch Busch was removed from the presidential palace. In April 1980, he was virtually imposed upon President Lidia Gueiler by the commanders of the garrison in La Paz in the face of strong opposition from Congress as well as opposition from several of the troop commanders in the provinces.

The election of May 1980 was almost a rerun of the one the year before. Once more, ex-President Siles came in with a plurality but not a majority, and Paz Estenssoro came in with the second highest number of votes, although a somewhat lesser proportion than he had had the year before.

However, in 1980 there was a significant difference from the situation the year before, a difference that might have assured the installation of a constitutional regime, but in fact turned out to be disastrous. In 1980, the supporters of Paz Estenssoro in Congress were ready to support the election of Siles as president of the Republic.

THE GARCÍA MEZA REGIME

The commander of the army, General García Meza, did not give Congress time to meet and elect Siles to the presidency. Raising the cry that Congress was about to choose a "leftist" as president, with disastrous consequences for the country, the general instigated a coup and installed himself in the presidential palace. Hundreds of people were arrested, including ex-President Paz Estenssoro, who was later moved to his hometown of Tarija where he was kept under house arrest, and Juan Lechín, who was kept in prison for about six months before being allowed to go into exile once again. Marcelo Quiroga Santa Cruz, one of the most promising of the younger political leaders, was murdered by the soldiers.

Siles succeeded in avoiding arrest and making his way abroad. There he proclaimed himself the legitimate constitutional president of the republic, and organized a kind of government in exile. He traveled extensively from his base in Ecuador, urging that other countries not recognize the usurping regime in La Paz and pressing his own claims to be the legitimate choice of the people of Bolivia.

There were certain peculiarities about this coup by the Bolivian army. First, elements of the Argentine military regime of General Jorge Videla were clearly associated with it. Some of the arrested trade unionists testified later that they had been interrogated not by Bolivian police or soldiers but by people with Argentine accents.

A second peculiar characteristic of the García Meza coup was the close relationship between those who carried it out and those in control of what was reputed to be a $2 billion a year cocaine trade. The Columbia Broadcasting System's weekly program "60 Minutes" ran twice during the winter and spring of 1981 a program concerning the role of the drug smugglers—including two members of García Meza's cabinet—in the new military government. There is ample evidence also from other sources concerning the importance of the drug smugglers in the García Meza regime, and some have argued that the major reason for the coup was fear on the part of the military personnel engaged in that trade that their operations might be interfered with by an elected civilian president, particularly such a notoriously honest one as Siles.

Third, this was probably the most sanguinary of the military regimes that held office in the years following the fall of the MNR government. Not only was Marcelo Quiroga Santa Cruz killed, but the same fate befell a number of labor leaders and lower ranking political figures. Torture and beatings were freely administered by the regime, presumably under direction of "experts" in these techniques brought in from Argentina.

The international reception of the García Meza coup was not friendly. Although the military regimes of Argentina and Brazil quickly recognized their counterpart in Bolivia, the United States and most of the democratic regimes of the hemisphere did not. Even with the advent in the United States in January 1981 of a conservative Republican administration, with an avowed policy of friendship for Latin American dictators, the García Meza government was not given official diplomatic recognition.

CONCLUSION

In August 1981, General García Meza was forced out of the presidency by his fellow officers. However, the drug smugglers continued to play a major role in the regime and in the armed forces. Some of the cocaine runners who had at first held cabinet and subcabinet positions had been removed from those overly exposed posts and placed in command of troops. One of the worst regimes in Bolivia's sad history continued in power.

8

BOLIVIAN POLITICS:
PAST AND PRESENT

Bolivia is still not really a modern nation. A substantial proportion of the country's population is scarcely aware (if it is aware at all) of the existence of Bolivia, and of their being an integral part of it. Bolivia barely has the territorial integration characteristic of a nation. There is no single language that all of the citizens recognize as the national lingua franca. Racial and cultural differences still divide the people of the republic into two (or more) groups having only marginal relations with one another.

However, the fact is that Bolivia has constituted a sovereign state for more than a century and a half. It has all of the formal attributes of such a state. It is internationally recognized as being a nation, since the fundamental juridical entity into which the contemporary world is divided is that of nation-states. Its government has all of the legal attributes of the ruling body of a nation, and the leaders of that government, regardless of how they have come to power, always speak in the name of "the nation."

In order to understand the politics of late twentieth-century Bolivia, one must take into account both of these aspects of the country's contemporary situation. The foregoing chapters have sought to do this by discussing the nature of the people of Bolivia, the land in which they live, and the economy that employs them as well as the historical evolution of the republic.

This chapter first sketches the formal structure of the Bolivian nation-state and then reviews again the main forces that influence national politics. This is followed by an assessment of the major effort that has been made to forge Bolivia into a modern nation—the Bolivian National Revolution. Finally, the relationship of Bolivia with the rest of the world is surveyed, ending with some speculation on the political future of Bolivia.

THE FORMAL STRUCTURE OF BOLIVIAN GOVERNMENT

Bolivia has something of a record among the Latin American countries in the number of constitutions that it has had since the first drawn up by Simón Bolívar during the country's first year of independence. The constitution of 1967, enacted by the regime of President Barrientos, is the country's sixteenth constitution.

The current document, like virtually all of its predecessors, provides for the standard three powers of government: the executive, the legislative, and the judicial. Basically copying the model of the constitution of the United States, the three branches of government are in theory of equal power. In practice, however, throughout most of the country's history the administrative branch has been overwhelmingly predominant.

The constitution provides for a president, as chief of the executive branch of government, to be elected every four years. Until 1962, the president was not eligible for reelection, but in that year this ineligibility was removed.

The president is empowered by the constitution to select the members of his cabinet. He can also choose the heads of the considerable number of autonomous or independent agencies, such as the Central Bank, the Development Corporation, the Agrarian Reform Institute, and many others.

The Bolivian president is officially commander-in-chief of the armed forces. Whether this is actually the case, however, has depended very much on the personality and individual power of a particular president, and the political circumstances within the armed forces at any given time.

The legislative branch of government consists of the National Congress. It is divided into two houses: a Senate consisting of 27 members, three from each of the country's nine departments; and a Chamber of Deputies of 102 members, elected on the basis of population.

As in the case of the United States, the vice-president of the republic is the presiding officer of the Senate. He is elected jointly with the president. In the case of the disappearance of the vice-president (as occurred in 1957 when Vice-President Ñuflo Chávez resigned), a president of the Senate elected by that body becomes its presiding officer and the constitutional successor of the president.

As in the case of the president, the members of the two legislative chambers are supposed to be elected by the citizenry. However, until 1952 that part of the citizenry having the right to vote was exceedingly limited, since only people who were literate and owned a certain minimum amount of property were electors. However, one of the first actions of the revolutionary government that seized power in April 1952 was to extend the right to vote to all Bolivians over 18 years of age, and this has not changed since then.

The president and Congress have their seats in La Paz. However, the third branch of the Bolivian government, the judiciary, has its headquarters in Sucre, which, under the name of Chuquisaca, was the former capital of the Spanish colonial dependency of Upper Peru and until 1899 the capital of Bolivia. The Supreme Court, according to the constitution, is supposed to be selected by the Congress, with a two-thirds vote necessary for anyone to be selected to the court. The Bolivian Supreme Court has two sections, criminal and civil, each of which has five justices, with the Chief Justice presiding over both. Under the Supreme Court are superior district courts with five to seven judges and local courts.

All three branches of the Bolivian national government preside over what is constitutionally a centralized, rather than a federal, state. The administrative subdivisions of Bolivia are the departments, of which there are nine. Their chief executives are named by the president of the republic, and there are no departmental legislatures. In no sense are the departments sovereign, although from time to time there have existed political movements in some of them, particularly in the department of Santa Cruz, that have advocated a wider degree of autonomy—if not independence—for the subdivisions of the republic.

As is the case in virtually all of the Spanish-American countries, the municipalities have little power. The mayors and councils of the cities and towns in Bolivia are elected, but the municipalities have very restricted authority and limited finances.

RELEVANCY AND IRRELEVANCY OF THE CONSTITUTION

Bolivian history indicates clearly that very few, if any, governments of the republic have adhered closely to the system of government established in the constitution. In even more or less democratically chosen administrations, the power of the executive branch of the government has certainly exceeded that which is formally granted by the constitution. In most of the governments, which have been dictatorships, the power of the executive has been overwhelming.

Even the dictatorships have by no means been oblivious to the constitution. In their decrees and decree-laws, the great majority cite some section or article of the existing constitution as the basis for whatever the legislation deals with, no matter how much that legislation may in fact violate the spirit, if not the letter, of the constitution.

It is also a fact that most of the Bolivian dictators have felt the need to "constitutionalize" their regimes, to convert them from de facto governments to de jure ones. The simplest way to do this has been to hold elections through which the dictator could be converted into a "constitutional president." Of course, to that end it has been necessary to ensure that the votes will be counted (if not cast) in such a way as to assure the "election" of the incumbent.

This process has sometimes involved pitfalls for the dictator. The most recent example is the situation faced by President Banzer when, after half a dozen years in power, he ultimately was forced by circumstances and his own promises to call elections. The very process of organizing elections created conditions that made it impossible for him to run at all, and finally resulted in his chosen successor not being able to maintain himself in power after his "victory" in patently fraudulent elections.

Quite a few Bolivian dictators have chosen a variation of the "constitutionalization" process. This has involved having an entirely new constitution written. In most cases, the changes made in the new document as compared to its predecessor are matters of detail, but they serve the purpose of giving certain prestige to the president currently in control. Of course, in most cases, the writing of a new constitution is followed by electing the current dictator as the "first constitutional president" under the new document, either by the constituent assembly that wrote it or by an election arranged soon afterward. In at least some instances, the individual involved has been the only constitutional president under that document because his successor has either reverted to an earlier constitution or has had a new one written on his behalf.

THE EVOLUTION OF BOLIVIAN GOVERNMENT AND POLITICS

The political organization of the Bolivian state has gone through several more or less clearly defined phases since Simón Bolívar created the republic more than a century and a half ago. These have been the period of caudillo rule, the domination of the oligarchy, the years of disintegration of oligarchical rule, the Bolivian National Revolution, and the military regime that has dominated the country since 1964.

Caudillismo was a characteristic of many of the Spanish-American nations for a longer or shorter period after the achievement of independence. It was a more or less natural result of the circumstances under which these countries achieved independence.

Bolivia, like the other Spanish-American colonies, had had virtually no institutions of self-government during the period in which it was dominated by the Spanish crown. All government and ecclesiastical officials in the colony owed their appointment either to the crown or to people appointed by the crown. Even the municipal *cabildos* that shared in the government of the cities had very limited powers and consisted of people who had either bought or inherited their positions. They in no real sense represented the people of their municipalities.

As a consequence, when Bolivia (and the other Spanish-American colonies) broke away from Spain, there were no "legitimate" authorities left. The situation was intensified by the fact that the Vatican took many years to recognize the independence of the new republic, and as a result, the influence of the Catholic Church, one of the legitimate sources of authority during the colonial period, was seriously weakened.

Given these circumstances, the only organized group that had a semblance of legitimacy left was the army of the new republic. Its source of authority was the fact that it had been responsible for bringing about the new dispensation.

The army soon degenerated into what some historians have called a force of occupation rather than a traditional national armed force. It quickly came to be dominated by charismatic individuals whose claim to power came to depend upon their ability to command the loyalty of enough armed men to assure them the ability to seize and maintain power, either locally in one part of the republic or in Bolivia as a whole.

The period of domination by the caudillos lasted in Bolivia from the ouster of President Sucre shortly after the establishment of the republic until the disastrous defeat of Bolivia in the War of the Pacific. That event marked the advent of the second period in Bolivian political history.

From the 1880s until the Chaco War of the 1930s, Bolivia was unquestionably dominated by the Rosca, a combination of the rural oligarchy and the mining interests. In spite of internal dissensions within the Rosca, there was little challenge during this half century to the domination of the country's economic and social elite.

Three different political groups were in control during this period. Between the early 1880s and 1899 the country was controlled by elements of the Conservative Party, more or less friendly to the Catholic Church and believing in government intervention in the economy. From 1899 until 1920, the Liberals were in command, dedicated to "free enterprise," unfriendly to the Church, and patronized particularly by the new tin-mining segment of the oligarchy.

After the coup of 1920, the Republicans were in charge of the government of Bolivia. Athough they included substantial numbers of the Rosca, they also had the backing of the artisan working class in La Paz and other cities. The dozen years before the Chaco War in 1932 were marked by the emergence of the first elements of a modern labor movement as well as of a young nationalist group among intellectuals that questioned the existing status quo.

The catastrophic defeat of Bolivia by Paraguay in the Chaco War (1932-35) seriously undermined the rule of the Rosca. For the first time, the young officers of the armed forces, which until then had been little more than the Praetorian Guard of the Rosca, began to question the domination of the agrarian-mining aristocracy. The principal spokesmen for this challenging attitude were Colonels David Toro and Germán Busch in the late 1930s and Major Gualberto Villarroel in the early 1940s. However, their short-lived regimes were able only to make a bare beginning at undermining the control of the Rosca on the country's economy, society, and politics. Nevertheless, they did bring into existence an organized labor movement, particularly in the mining camps, that was to play a major role in the country's development in later years.

The major changes in Bolivia came during the revolutionary years of 1952–64. Under the leadership of the Movimiento Nacionalista Revolucionario, the government of that period brought about very fundamental changes. It gave the land back to the Indians, the most basic change that could be brought about in the republic, nationalized the "big three" tin-mining enterprises, and started a process of economic development, particularly in the Oriente.

In the last half of the MNR regime, however, it revived the traditional armed forces, which it had first dissolved, and in November 1964 the military overthrew the revolutionary government. Since then, the soldiers have dominated the government of Bolivia and still determine who shall govern Bolivia.

REASONS FOR THE PARTIAL SUCCESS OF THE REVOLUTIONARY GOVERNMENT

The most important question concerning contemporary Bolivian politics is why the MNR regime was not able to establish firmly a pattern of stable civilian government. The answer is not a simple one. The revolutionary administrations carried out many of the objectives of the Movimiento Nacionalista Revolucionario, but their most spectacular failure was in ending the pattern of military government from which Bolivia has suffered during a large part of its history.

An outside observer might expect that the MNR regime had established a wide enough range of civilian support that it would be able to exert control over the armed forces. However, although this appeared to be the case during the first half dozen years of the revolutionary government, it was proved in the process of the regime's term in office that massive popular support was not enough to maintain the revolutionary government.

The MNR government came into power with the strong support of the well-organized miners, the manual workers of the major cities, and most of the white-collar workers. As a result of the government's encouragement of the organization of the peasants and of the agrarian reform, it won the overwhelming allegiance of the rural population.

During the late 1950s there was considerable popularity for the idea that the MNR was on the way to developing a system similar to that of Mexico, in which the party standing for the revolution completely dominated the country's politics and controlled its government with only minor opposition. However, this did not prove to be correct.

There are at least six reasons for the failure of the Bolivian MNR to develop into a party like the Partido Revolucionario Institucional of Mexico, and thus save Bolivia from the militarism that succeeded the MNR regime. These are: the alienation of the miners, the decline of the peasant militia, too great development of the traditional military, U.S. pressure, the weakness of the Bolivian economy, and finally internal dissension within the MNR.

The alienation of the miners from the revolutionary regime was almost inevitable. As indicated earlier, the revolutionary government (as would any government of Bolivia) needed to use the surpluses created by the mining industry to foster the development of the rest of the economy. Sooner or later, therefore, it would have had to quarrel with the miners over the amount of this surplus that was being taken by the miners, their union, and its leaders. It would also have to try to make the mining industry more efficient, so that it would bring in more income (and particularly foreign exchange) to the government's coffers. Both of these measures would inevitably arouse a considerable degree of resistance on the part of the miners' unions. By the beginning of the 1960s, such resistance was clear.

The alienation of the miners would not have been so serious for the MNR regime if at the same time it had continued to maintain the strength of the peasant militia, which by the early 1960s had come to be the major paramilitary support of the regime. However, it did not do so, for several reasons.

First, the development of the peasant organizations—unions, militia units, and party branches—had given rise to a considerable number of caciques, local Indian leaders, who in time came to be more concerned with strengthening their own local power bases than with supporting the MNR regime. This dispersion of power among the peasant population very much weakened the ability of the MNR government to use the peasant militia to defend the regime.

Second, the failure of the MNR regime to go beyond the mere transfer of land to the Indians also weakened the revolutionary government. Once the Indians received the land, they became concerned principally with making certain that they would never lose it, and became willing to support any government that would assure this. The MNR government did not go ahead to develop sufficiently other kinds of relationships between it and the mass of the Indian peasants—credit facilities, technical assistance, aid in marketing their products—that might have tied them more closely to the revolutionary regime.

Had the revolutionary government developed a series of programs for providing the kinds of services the peasants needed to expand the productivity of their farms and to help them enter more fully into the monetized sector of the Bolivian economy, the role of the peasant caciques would have been quite different. As intermediaries between the peasantry on the one hand and the government that was extending aid to their peasant constituents on the other, the caciques would have continued to have a vested interest in strengthening the MNR government and keeping it in power. Their ability to maintain positions of leadership among the peasants would have depended mainly on their ability to work effectively with the national government for the purpose of obtaining things for their constituents.

Thus, the cohesion of the revolutionary government and of the MNR party organization would have been more strongly maintained. However, as it was, once the Indians under the leadership of any particular cacique had obtained their land, there was little reason for that cacique to continue to stand in well with the national regime, and both the caciques and those whom they more or less represented had less and less immediate interest in the maintenance of the revolutionary government, so long as its successor did not threaten to take away their landholdings.

An additional aspect of this situation was that the MNR government took the support of the peasant militia too much for granted. Apparently in the last few years of the regime, very little attention was paid in La Paz to assuring that the peasant militia continued its training, had sufficient arms to help the government in the case of an emergency, and had an organizational structure that could assure its quick mobilization.

As a result of these factors, by the early 1960s the peasant militia support for the MNR regime had been fatally undermined. When the party and the government tried to rally them to the support of the administration of President Paz Estenssoro in November 1964, such support was not forthcoming.

THE ROLE OF THE ARMED FORCES

A third factor that undermined the government of the MNR was the decision to revive the traditional military. Although the regime sought to bring back into the army and other services only those officers unquestionably loyal to the MNR, it was not successful in doing so. A number of officers, including, for example, Alfredo Ovando, who by 1964 was a general, had never had a close relationship with the MNR. However, even more fateful was the fact that many of the military men who were supposedly loyal to the regime and belonged to the party, such as General René Barrientos, finally turned against the revolutionary party and government.

In addition, the government of President Hernán Siles and the second administration of Paz Estenssoro armed the traditional military to a degree that was politically dangerous and ultimately fatal. The new armament sharply shifted the balance of force between the traditional military and the various civilian militia groups, strongly in favor of the former. As a result, when the showdown came, the traditional military had little to challenge them insofar as force was concerned.

The building up of the traditional armed forces was in large part due to pressure from the United States. Beginning a couple years after the start of the revolution, the United States gave very extensive economic aid to the revolutionary government. This gave considerable leverage to urge that the armed forces be greatly strengthened. All of the armament that the reconstituted military received came from the United States. The United States government clearly was not particularly concerned with whether the relatively heavy arming of the Bolivian army, navy, and air force would undermine the civilian government. On the other hand, both the U.S. embassy and the officials in the United States were very much worried about the Bolivian government's dependency to such a high degree on civilian militia of various kinds.

An additional important element in the situation was the innate weakness of the Bolivian economy. This weakness made the need for nationalizing the mining industry much more pressing than it might otherwise have been, and it also made the revolutionary government much more dependent than was healthy on help from the United States government. It likewise made it more difficult to control inflationary pressures and to bring about increases in the level of living of the country's urban population than would have been the case if the economy had been stronger and more prosperous.

THE PROBLEM OF MNR DISUNITY

Finally, the most decisive factor in the failure of the MNR to develop into a Bolivian version of the Mexican PRI was the tendency of the party to splinter. As a result of this, key leaders and substantial popular groups that had originally been backers of the MNR ended up as supporters of the move to oust the revolutionary government.

Although, as indicated earlier, there was in the beginning a strong feeling of esprit de corps and loyalty to the party, and very few real ideological differences among the top leaders of the MNR, personal rivalries among those leaders later wrenched the party asunder. In the first years of the revolution, it appeared as if there was general agreement that the four top figures in the MNR would each be assured his turn in the presidency of the republic. It has even been said that the order in which they would succeed one another had been worked out and agreed to: Paz Estenssoro, Siles, Walter Guevara Arze, and Lechín, in that order.

However, if there was such an agreed-to schedule of presidencies, it was not adhered to, at least not after the first change in government. Siles did succeed Paz Estenssoro in 1956, but when it came time for Walter Guevara Arze to take the place of Siles, the rotational system broke down.

Admittedly, there was considerable opposition within the MNR to the succession of Walter Guevara Arze to the presidency. He was looked upon as representing the Right within the party, and therefore, as one who would continue the economic stabilization policies launched by President Siles, who in those days also had the reputation of being in the right wing of the party—whatever that meant in the Bolivian context.

In the face of this opposition, which was undoubtedly particularly strong among the miners, who had been especially unhappy about the stabilization policies of the Siles regime, the "perfect" solution for the election of 1960 seemed to be the reelection of Paz Estenssoro. He was without question the first among the equals who made up the top leadership of the party. Furthermore, he was considered as not belonging to either the Right or the Left within the party. The only major figure within the party who disagreed with this "perfect" choice of the MNR candidate was Walter Guevara Arze, who led the first important, albeit not very large, split in the party to form his own Partido Revolucionario Autentico.

Much more serious was the controversy over the 1964 party nomination. There is no question about the fact that Lechín had been promised the MNR candidacy for that year. The reason he did not receive it is still a subject of controversy.

The opponents of Paz Estenssoro within and outside the MNR attribute the failure to nominate Lechín and the decision that Paz Estenssoro should run once again to Paz Estenssoro's own enjoyment of power and the presidency. One of their principal pieces of evidence to sustain this argument is that the constitution was altered in 1962 to permit the immediate reelection of the incumbent president, something which until then had been forbidden.

However, Paz Estenssoro himself argues that the decision not to run Lechín for the presidency in 1964 was taken as the result of very strong pressure from the United States government. According to his version of events, the U.S. authorities told him that if Lechín were to become president, all further economic aid to the Bolivian government would be ended. There is at least some evidence that would lend credence to this version of events. It is certainly true that the United States authorities never really understood Lechín and his position in national politics. He tended to be pictured as a far leftist, perhaps because within the miners' federation he had had traditionally to get along with both Trotskyist and Stalinist elements that had substantial influence within the Federación Sindical de Trabajadores Mineros.

The fact was, however, that Lechín was as loyal a "movimientista" as any of the other principal leaders of the MNR. He was, for sure, a person who (if he could acquire it) preferred to have power without too much responsibility. He had demonstrated this on various occasions by being conveniently out of the country in moments of crisis.

However, as president of the republic, Lechín could not have avoided responsibility. Furthermore, he had considerable support, particularly among the miners, but also among other working-class groups. If he had been elected president with the backing of the other principal figures of the MNR, he would also have had the backing of the mass of the peasantry, and the catastrophic splintering of the MNR that took place in 1964 would have been avoided.

The 1964 crisis was fatal to the party and the revolutionary government. Not only did it result in Lechín's withdrawal from the MNR with his followers to form the rival PRIN, but it also brought about the defection of many secondary figures who regarded Paz Estenssoro's third nomination as an attempt to obtain personalist control of the party.

Finally, the 1964 crisis gave the military a chance to reassert a political role, at first within the party, and then against it. Paz Estenssoro's first nominee for his running mate in the 1964 election, a civilian, although nominated by a party convention, was soon forced to withdraw. In his place, the head of the "military cells" of the party, air force General René Barrientos, was substituted for him. Many MNR leaders and nonparty people looked upon Barrientos' nomination with great distrust, feeling that it was (as proved to be the case) exceedingly dangerous to submit to military pressure on behalf of one of the country's principal armed forces leaders.

In the last analysis, it was this splintering of the MNR that doomed the party and the revolutionary government. A united party enjoying the support of the great majority of the civilian population might well have been able to offer effective resistance to any military bid for control. A greatly weakened MNR, abandoned by all but one of its principal figures, was in no position to offer such resistance.

THE ELEMENTS OF POWER UNDER THE MILITARY REGIME

The upshot of the events of 1964 was the installation of a more thoroughly militarist regime than Bolivia had at any time since the age of the caudillos. Of course, it has differed from the militarism of the caudillo period in that the dictatorships since 1964 have been representative of the armed forces as a corporative unit, rather than impositions by any charismatic leader supported by his personal followers under arms. With the possible exception of Barrientos, none of the military presidents since 1964 has been a charismatic figure. In most instances, succession to the presidency has had a strong hierarchical tinge, with the man temporarily in the highest place in the hierarchy taking advantage of that fact to install himself in the presidential palace on the Plaza Murillo.

Thus, the most decisive element in national politics since 1964 has been the armed forces. However, it has by no means been the only element of power during this period. For one thing, the military has often split, and upon various occasions it has had to retreat in the face of very strong pressure from the civilians.

In addition to the military, at least seven other elements in national politics have exerted varying degrees of power at different times in the period since 1964. These are the governmental bureaucracy, the "middle mining" sector, peasant groups, the unions, the political parties, university students and the Roman Catholic Church.

The governmental bureaucracy and within it a new group of technocrats have exercised considerable power, particularly in determining national economic policy. The Bolivia of the early 1980s is fundamentally different from the Bolivia of a generation ago in having a small but substantial group of more or less well-trained experts in the social sciences and related fields in the public administration. These include economists, sociologists, management experts, and other technocrats.

Since the military, which has generally held the top positions in the government since 1964, is admittedly quite ignorant about the details of running even as modern an economy as Bolivia now possesses, it has tended to turn these matters over to the technocrats, no matter who occupies the presidency. It is these people who have generally made the decisions—usually ratified by the general who for the moment occupies the presidency—concerning such matters as economic development policy, tariff protection, monetary policy, and the negotiation of loans from abroad. They also have often been heard on such matters as labor policy and other clearly political concerns.

Another new factor in the power equation of Bolivia that has appeared since 1964 is the so-called "middle mining" sector. When the "big three" mining companies were nationalized by the revolutionary regime in 1952, other private mine owners were left alone, including several foreign firms that operated in the country at the time. Since the private mine owners have proven to be much more efficient in running their enterprises than has COMIBOL, the state firm, their part of the total output of the mining industry has tended to grow slowly but steadily. This is particularly true of the firms which, although smaller than COMIBOL, were large enough to be able to afford considerable investment in their enterprises. As a result, the political power of these "middle" firms has tended to grow. It was commonly said that they were a major element in the political calculations of the Banzer government that controlled the country during most of the 1970s.

The peasants also remain a political power to be calculated with. This is attested to by the insistence of most of the military dictators since 1964 on negotiating a renewal of the "peasant-military pact," which President Barrientos first signed. Often the peasant leaders who signed such renewals of the "pact" were more or less selected by the military, but the very fact that the armed forces leaders felt it necessary to at least go through the motions of asserting their alliance with the peasants has been a tacit recognition of the potential power that the peasants still possess.

The military regimes have sought to limit this power as much as possible. They have made sure that no civilian political groups would be free to agitate among and organize the peasants, as the MNR had done during the revolutionary period. At the same time, the military has undoubtedly sought to play various peasant leaders off against each other, stimulating the "caciquism" that grew out of the early peasant union movement. They have also seen to it that the peasant militia remains nothing more than a memory.

On the other hand, the military regimes have all been careful not to touch the major benefit that the peasants received from the revolutionary governments—control over the land of the Altiplano and the Yungas. The peasants have thus generally been willing to tolerate any general who happens at any given time to be passing through the presidential palace. At the same time, they have been more or less content to continue their ages-long isolation from the rest of the Bolivian nation as the surest means of protecting themselves from exploitation by the mestizo and the white man.

The labor unions have also continued to maintain at least some political power. In spite of the efforts of some of the military presidents to suppress or depoliticize them, and of others to co-opt them, the unions have continued to exist, to assert as much independence from government control as a given situation 'permits, and to take advantage of any crisis to reassert their rights and political power.

Undoubtedly, the unions' high point of influence after 1964 was during the government of General Torres (1970-71) when they formed the Popular Assembly, which aspired to function as a kind of dual power soviet on the 1917 Russian model. However, at other times, too, the unions have asserted themselves very strongly, particularly during the last months of the Banzer government in 1977-78.

The miners remain the most significant of the labor gorups. Their long record of militancy and strategic position of being able at any given time to cripple the major source of the country's exports has made them continue to be a force to be reckoned with. This is attested to by the frequency with which the military presidents have found it "necessary" to invade the mining camps with army units.

The political parties continue to have some influence. As in the case of the unions, despite efforts of the various military regimes either to suppress them or buy them off, the political parties have been able to bounce back whenever an opportunity to do so presented itself.

Remarkably little has changed in the mosaic of political parties since 1964. There is no doubt that the MNR (including its several factions) remains overwhelmingly the most popular party in the country. At least until 1978, the Falange Socialista Boliviana constituted its principal right-wing opposition among the parties, and there continued to be—as before 1964—a much splintered conglomeration of parties to the Left of the MNR.

The most significant fact about the parties since 1964, as was the case at the end of the revolutionary period, is the inability of the MNR to close its ranks, and thus to form what would certainly be a major challenge to the continuation of the military in power. Since 1971, the principal division in the MNR ranks has been that between the followers of Paz Estenssoro, who have at various times called themselves just the MNR and the Historic MNR, and that of the backers of Hernán Siles, who has since 1971 headed the MNR of the Left, the MNRI. In three successive elections in 1978, 1979, and 1980, these two men, backed by their own MNR factions and various smaller groups allied to them, were the principal civilian contenders for the presidency. Certainly between them they got the vast majority of the votes in all three cases.

However, the inability of the two major branches of the MNR to sink their differences led to the two years of indecision and three successive elections of the 1978–80 period. Ironically, it was the final agreement of the Paz Estenssoro forces in Congress to support the choice of Siles in 1980 that provoked the army coup of that year which put in power the cocaine-smuggling regime of President García Meza.

One party shift of some significance has taken place on the right wing of national politics. This has been the rise of a party headed by former President Hugo Banzer as the principal spokesman for the Right in the elections of 1979 and 1980. In assuming this position, it has co-opted the situation held for three decades by the Falange Socialista Boliviana, which in part because of its own internal dissension has been reduced to a minor force in national party politics.

To a considerable degree, the political parties are dominated in the early 1980s by the same people who led them before 1964. However, individuals like Paz Estenssoro, Siles, Guevara Arze, Lechín, and the leaders of the Falange and of many of the small leftist parties are approaching—if they have not reached—old age. There is not any clearly defined next generation of leadership on the horizon, particularly in the two major factions of the MNR.

A few younger party leaders of significance did appear after 1964, principally in the smaller parties. One such figure, Marcelo Quiroga Santa Cruz, head of the Socialist Party, was unfortunately murdered at the time of the García Meza coup in 1980. However, one of the more promising groups of young political figures is to be found in the MIR, which originated as a division in the Christian Democratic Party in the late 1960s and a decade later was closely associated with Siles' faction of the MNR.

The university students, particularly those of the University of San Andrés in La Paz, have had some political power also since 1964. Through strikes, demonstrations, and riots they have embarrassed and sometimes even endangered the government in power at any given moment. The leverage of the La Paz students has been more than it might otherwise have been because of the location of the university right in the center of the city, only a few blocks from the presidential palace. However, the influence of the students is only likely to be significant if the organized workers and all or most of the political parties are also determined to challenge the regime in power. The students generally tend to stand considerably to the Left of most of the other elements in national politics.

Finally, mention should be made of the political significance of the Catholic Church in post-1964 Bolivia. The church has for most of the twentieth century not been a major factor in national politics. However, in recent years, influenced by Pope John XXIII and his successors, and by the Vatican Council and trends in the church within Latin America, the Bolivian Catholic Church has begun to play a more significant role. It was of major importance in bringing the Banzer regime to an end in 1977–78 because of the support it gave to those who were conducting passive resistance against that government. It may be expected to continue to speak out for human rights and against the abysmal corruption that has come to characterize the military regimes.

9

FOREIGN RELATIONS

Before attempting to speculate on the proximate future of Bolivian politics, it is important to say a word about the country's relations with the rest of world. Although Bolivia still remains relatively isolated, it is certainly influenced by what is happening with its immediate neighbors and by its relations with those neighbors as well as by what is occurring in the world beyond Bolivia's immediate environment.

As noted at various times, during its more than a century and a half of independence, Bolivia has lost substantial amounts of territory to all of its immediate neighbors: Chile, Peru, Brazil, Paraguay, and Argentina. Perhaps one of the surprising things about Bolivian politics, therefore, is the fact that with only one exception, there exists virtually no revanchist feeling against these neighbors. The exception, of course, is Chile. Bolivia, officially, and in the feelings of most of its politically conscious citizens, has never given up aspiration to regain access to the Pacific Ocean. This can only be achieved at the expense of Chile.

As a result of this situation, relations with Chile are always somewhat precarious. During the last quarter of a century, diplomatic relations between the two countries have been suspended on various occasions. Although early in the Banzer administration, soon after General Pinochet had seized power in Chile, relations warmed and it seemed possible that the old contention might be settled, this proved to be an illusion. It is not likely that in the near future really friendly relations will be established between the two countries.

In recent years, the influence of both Brazil and Argentina on Bolivian internal affairs has grown substantially. In part, this is a reflection of the withdrawal of the United States from its role of principal provider of economic and military aid to the country, and in part, too, of the general decline of U.S. influence in Latin America, creating a kind of vacuum that in this part of the region has been at least partially filled by Bolivia's two largest neighbors.

It is generally accepted that the Brazilian government played a major role in the conquest of power by Colonel Banzer in 1971. A safe staging area for his uprising and financial help was undoubtedly provided by the Brazilian military regime at that time. Subsequently, Brazilian economic penetration in Bolivia increased substantially.

Similarly, the coup organized by General García Meza in 1980 was undoubtedly aided and abetted by the Argentine military government of General Jorge Videla. Subsequent to it, Argentine police agents almost certainly cooperated with police of the García Meza government in persecuting the civilian opposition. Argentina almost immediately extended diplomatic recognition to the new installment of the Bolivian military dictatorship.

Relations with Paraguay and Peru have generally been friendly, if somewhat distant, in recent decades. However, after the García Meza coup, there was some fear in Peru that the Bolivian military might try to encourage (perhaps with the aid of the Argentine and possibly the Brazilian regimes), a move to overthrow the recently elected civilian government of President Fernando Belaúnde Terry.

Bolivia belongs to the Andean Bloc with Venezuela, Colombia, Ecuador, and Peru. Chile at first belonged but withdrew soon after the military dictatorship of General Pinochet was established there. The purpose of the bloc is to establish a full common market among its members, with the removal of barriers to trade among these members, and the establishment of a common protective barrier around the bloc as a whole.

Bolivia is economically the weakest of the members of the bloc, and it is provided with special rights to maintain protection for certain kinds of goods for several years after the other members have removed these barriers. Bolivia has been assigned certain branches of the metal-mechanical, petrochemical, and auto parts industries, in accordance with the Andean Bloc policy of allocating different lines of industrial development to the various members of the bloc.

Trade has increased modestly with the other members of the Andean Bloc. However, it has increased even more with Brazil and Argentina, which, as comparatively industrialized countries, have a growing demand for the raw materials produced in Bolivia.

Although there has been some agitation, which reached a high point after García Meza's coup, for Bolivia to withdraw from the Andean Bloc, it has not done so. The potential markets for Bolivian agricultural and mineral exports within the bloc, which includes some 60 million people, are attractive, and at the same time the assignment of new manufacturing industries in Bolivia by the bloc may go far to offset whatever damage to older industries is incurred by having to lower protective barriers against imports from other bloc members.

For half a century or more, Bolivian relations with the United States have been of major significance, at least for Bolivia. As early as 1936, the administration of Franklin D. Roosevelt failed to apply the "big stick" policy when the government of President David Toro expropriated the holdings of the Standard Oil Company of New Jersey, thus marking an early application of the Good Neighbor Policy. Subsequently, the U.S. government brought considerable pressure on Standard Oil to accept a settlement of the compensation issue that was not unfavorable to Bolivia. In the years immediately following, the United States government had considerable preoccupation with supposedly extensive German penetration in Bolivia, but the governments of General Quintanilla and Peñaranda in the early 1940s cooperated with the United States in restricting whatever German influence there was in the country, and developed close working relations with the United States.

The period of closest relations was that between 1953 and the death of President Barrientos in 1969. During the period of the revolutionary regime, the United States had a major economic aid program for Bolivia, and at one point it was the largest such program per capita anywhere in the world. Economic aid included food grants, financing and technical aid for specific programs in transportation, agriculture and other fields, and general budget support funds. Beginning with the second Paz Estenssoro administration, it also helped in the program of reorganization and rationalization of the tin-mining industry, generally known as the Triangular Plan.

These close relations continued, if at a somewhat lower intensity, during the administration of President Barrientos. However, by the end of that period, both the nature of the Ovando and Torres governments and the general decline in U.S. economic aid to Latin America reduced the closeness of the Bolivian regime to the United States. By the 1970s, as indicated, Brazil and Argentina had begun to step in to exert influence that the United States was relinquishing.

Trade contacts, if not other kinds of relationships, have been growing with a number of areas outside of America. Traditionally, most of the country's tin has been sold to the major tin market in Great Britain, but in more recent years, trade has grown with such unexpected areas as South Korea, Taiwan, and Hong Kong. Even the People's Republic of China now appears as one of Bolivia's trading partners, albeit not a major one.

A special word might be said about relations with the Soviet Union. At various times the USSR has shown a flickering interest in Bolivia. On several occasions in the late 1950s and the 1960s, it offered to build a tin smelter for Bolivia, an offer that was firmly if politely rejected. Bolivia has had very little that the Soviet Union wanted to sell, and the Bolivians have generally preferred to buy elsewhere what might also be available from the Soviet Union. As a result, trade between the two countries has not attained any significance for either side.

Relations with the Soviet Union took an interesting turn under the García Meza regime. Of course, the USSR has for 40 years had a "representative" in

Bolivia in the form of a political party loyal to the Soviet Union, first the PIR and then, after 1950, the Communist Party of Bolivia (Partido Communista de Bolivia—PCB). The PCB has never become a major force in the country's politics, although having some influence in the miners' unions. It has suffered the same ups and downs of all the other parties since 1964. However, after the seizure of power by García Meza this situation seemed to change.

This change came because of the close relations between the García Meza military regime and that of Argentina. The Argentine military government maintained very friendly relations with the Soviet Union, which became Argentina's most important trading partner, as well as entering into contracts for a number of economic development projects in Argentina. At the same time, the Argentine Communist Party was virtually untouched by the military regime, which substantially repressed several of the country's other parties, and the Soviet Union never attacked the extensive violations of human rights by the Argentine regime, in sharp contrast of the Soviet attitude toward similar events in General Pinochet's Chile.

After García Meza's coming to power, this Argentine-Soviet relationship seemed to be extended to relations between Bolivia and the USSR. On the one hand, the García Meza government arrested almost no members of the pro-Soviet Communist Party, whereas it was jailing, torturing, and killing members of virtually all other parties. For its part, the Soviet Union virtually ignored the violent suppression of the opposition by García Meza as well as the notorious participation by leaders of the García Meza regime in the international narcotics trade.

It is not clear now whether this somewhat peculiar relationship will develop into a broader pattern of cooperation between the Bolivian government and the Soviet government and its "affiliate" in Bolivia. However, it does represent a rather strange—if minor—twist in Bolivian international relations.

10

THE OUTLOOK

It is perilous in the extreme to make any hard and fast predictions about the future of politics in Bolivia. Governments are prone to change with such rapidity and sometimes in such unexpected directions that it is hazardous to postulate specific predictions of future trends.

However, it is possible to suggest some factors that are likely to be of key importance in determining Bolivia's political future. These include at least the following: the degree to which a new leadership emerges among the civilian politicians and parties; the progress of general economic development; the rapidity with which the Indians are integrated with the rest of the population and develop interests and demands beyond that of merely being left alone to cultivate the land that they have now possessed for more than a generation; the degree to which Bolivia is subject to outside intervention, particularly from its two powerful neighbors, Brazil and Argentina; and the long-run effects of the cocaine-smugglers' regime which took power in 1980.

If there is to be any hope for political democracy in Bolivia, there must emerge new leadership among the civilian political party leaders. New people are needed with new ideas of how to build on the accomplishments of the Bolivian National Revolution in order to meld together the two major components of the Bolivian population into a real nation and to develop a more productive and equitable economy. No such leaders are clearly visible at the moment. However, this is not to say that they do not exist. When the next turn of the political wheel comes—and it is again the chance of the civilian political leaders to play at least a major, if not the dominant, part in national politics—

such leadership may well emerge. Certain potential figures exist in the two major coalitions that gathered around the two principal MNR factions in the 1978, 1979, and 1980 elections. Hopefully, their time will come the next time around.

Of key importance, too, is the continued sound economic development of the country. The further expansion of the new economy in the Oriente, the expansion of transportation facilities among the three geographical areas of the country, some degree of industrialization, perhaps based on the allocation decisions of the Andean Bloc or on the beginning of the exploitation of the Motún iron deposits, will help the process of welding Bolivia together as a nation. Economic development, too, will make more possible a rising level of living for the masses of the populace that will certainly not assure but may well facilitate the emergence of a democratic polity.

Certainly of key significance for the political future of the country will be the degree to which the Indian, who still constitutes the majority of the population, is integrated into the money economy, develops new needs and aspirations that force the politicians—civilian or military—to push more rapidly the task of his transformation from a subsistence farmer into a more or less modern agriculturalist, and is converted from a passive into an active citizen. As has been indicated several times, the political leaders of the last three decades have been all but oblivious of the task of integration of the Indian into the modern economy and society and the importance of this task for the emergence of a true Bolivian nation.

Of significance, too, will be the degree to which Bolivia succeeds in avoiding domination by one or another of its much stronger neighbors. It is almost certain that there are political developments in Bolivia that neither Brazil nor Argentina will want to permit. However, much will depend upon how wide or narrow a definition the military rulers of Brazil and Argentina (or even their possible civilian successors) will give to the things that are deemed to be nonpermissible. It will depend, also, on the willingness and ability of Bolivian leaders to resist these pressures from across their eastern and southern frontiers.

Finally, of key importance will be the question of how much long-run damage the cocaine-smuggling government that took power in 1980 has done to the country. Drug smuggling mushroomed into an activity that overshadowed all other aspects of the economy, and for the time being at least, gave the military rulers a relatively free hand both in dealing with other economic interests inside the country and with foreign powers that might want to influence the trend of events within Bolivia. It threatened, also, to convert vast sections of the republic from production of foods and fibers to the cultivation of the coca plant, undoubtedly intensifying an already unhealthy dependence upon imported foodstuffs.

The predominance of the drug smugglers has also greatly aggravated a problem that Bolivia has always had—that of corruption. Since the very nature of the drug trade is corruption, and since it was practiced by the highest officials of the Bolivian government, the effect was to make corruption in the government service all but universal.

It is difficult to foresee just what the long-term results of all of this will be. On the one hand, it may serve to keep the thoroughly corrupted segment of the military leadership in power for a long time, giving them both the resources with which to buy off opponents and the motivation to be absolutely ruthless toward those opponents who will not cooperate.

On the other hand, the triumph of the cocaine-dealing elements within the Bolivian army may have quite the opposite results. It may conceivably engender a shame and feeling of disgrace among the less venal and more patriotic members of the armed forces leadership that will bring them to end what is without question an international disgrace for Bolivia. It may also serve to discredit the military so that they will be forced to "return to the barracks" for a long time. Both civilians and military personnel may come to the conclusion that no civilian regime has ever been as bad or done as much to undermine and disgrace the nation as have the generals, colonels, and their underlings who first triumphed with García Meza. If this is the reaction, the long-run effects of the experience may well be positive.

In any case, the task of building a real Bolivian nation remains. A major step was taken in this direction by the Bolivian National Revolution. Some progress toward it has been made since then. The future drama of Bolivian politics will be carried out fundamentally within this context of forging a single nation out of the still dispersed and divided Bolivian people.

BIBLIOGRAPHICAL NOTE

Many of the observations on the recent and contemporary scene in Bolivia that are contained in this book are the result of the author's own observations and conversations with a broad range of informants. However, a number of sources have been consulted for statistical material and historical information.

First, a word about sources of statistics. It has been said about Latin American countries, including Bolivia, that "statistics are poetry." As noted earlier in this volume, there is not even any general agreement on the size of Bolivia's territory and certainly not on the number of people in the country.

My policy with regard to statistical materials, therefore, has been to consult standard sources, and where they agree concerning a particular piece of data, to use that information. In cases in which there is disagreement, I have either indicated this, using the figure that seemed most reasonable, or have indicated the range of disagreement. The principal standard sources involved have been the *Stateman's Year Book 1980/1981*, *Academic American Encyclopedia*, the most recent *Encyclopedia Britannica*, and *The World Almanac and Book of Facts 1981*.

For readers who are interested in more detail on specific aspects of Bolivia, the following volumes, which I have consulted, would be of interest:

Alexander, Robert J. *The Bolivian National Revolution*. New Brunswick: Rutgers University Press, 1958.

Fifer, J. Valerie. *Bolivia: Land, Location and Politics Since 1825*. Cambridge, England: Cambridge University Press, 1972. Concentrates particularly on geography, but also has considerable historical, cultural, and other material.

Klein, Herbert S. *Parties and Political Change in Bolivia, 1880-1952*. Cambridge, England: Cambridge University Press, 1969. Very useful for the parties and general political history before the Bolivian National Revolution.

Lora, Guillermo. *A History of the Bolivian Labor Movement*. Cambridge, England: Cambridge University Press, 1977. A very useful compilation and translation of a four-volume work by the major Trotskyist leader of Bolivia.

Malloy, James M. *Bolivia: The Uncomplete Revolution*. Pittsburgh: Pittsburgh University Press, 1970. A very interesting overview of the Bolivian National Revolution, very informative, although I do not agree with all of Malloy's interpretations of events.

Malloy, James M., and Richard Thorn, eds. *Beyond the Revolution: Bolivia Since 1952*. Pittsburgh: Pittsburgh University Press.

Mitchell, Christopher. *The Legacy of Populism in Bolivia: From the MNR to Military Rule*. New York: Praeger, 1977.

Osborne, Harold. *Bolivia, A Land Divided*. New York and London: Royal Institute of International Affairs, 1954. Certainly the best short overall view of the country in print.

Ostria Gutierrez, Alberto. *A People Crucified: The Tragedy of Bolivia*. New York: Prestige Book, 1958. A study of the Bolivian National Revolution by one of its most bitter opponents.

For certain details of history, anthropology, archeology, and other matters, I have consulted books that deal with Latin America rather than specifically with Bolivia. The most significant are those of John A. Crow, *The Epic of Latin America* (Garden City, Long Island: Doubleday, 1971), and Nicolás Sánchez-Albórnoz, *The Population of Latin America: A History* (Berkeley: University of California Press, 1974).

Finally, mention must be made of the article on Bolivia that appeared in the eleventh edition of the *Encyclopedia Britannica*, vol. 4 (New York, 1910). It has one of the most detailed descriptions on the geology, geography, and related matters in Bolivia, and a highly interesting description of the socio-economic situation in the country at the beginning of the twentieth century that provides an invaluable backdrop for the changes which have occurred in the country since that time.

INDEX

ABOUT THE AUTHOR

ROBERT J. ALEXANDER is a professor of economics and political science at Rutgers University. He has published 25 books, most of them dealing with Latin America, including *The Bolivian National Revolution*, the first English-language study of that upheaval.